What's Gaby Cooking

GRILLING

all the things

What's Gaby Cooking

ING
the things

100+ Recipes to Make You an Absolute Pro

Gaby Dalkin

Abrams, New York

CONTENTS

INTRODUCTION

The complete irony of this book—which is dedicated to demystifying and simplifying all things grilling—is that it was born of total and utter chaos. It was 2021 (enough said); we were in the middle of renovating our kitchen down to the studs; and I was pregnant with Poppy. Plus, in the thick of all that, I still needed to deliver all the tasty recipes to the What's Gaby Cooking community, not to mention just make dinner for Thomas and me. So when I found myself on a mission to perfect a frittata but had no oven available, I threw it—cast-iron pan and all—on the grill. And it was perfection.

I'm no stranger to some smoky, charred-in-all-the-right-ways open-fire cooking. But what I realized with that frittata-fueled epiphany was how underutilized the grill is for quick, easy everyday preparations. Though it looks a little different than an oven or stovetop, it's more similar than you might think—you adjust the heat according to what you're cooking, and you close the lid for an ovenlike effect or leave it open for a stovetop one (and with a fraction of the cleanup because you're not dealing with roasting pans or oil-filled skillets)—so I wanted to get to the heart of why more of us aren't out there enjoying the fresh air and taking advantage of all that extra flavor that's there for the taking.

I started thinking about all the things I hear when I'm cooking out with friends or when I post grilling recipes on my platform: "Grilling seems so complicated," or "I don't know where to start," or "I don't eat meat, so it doesn't really seem like it's for me." And after doing an even deeper dive into all the things about grilling that people get hung up on, I decided to put together the ultimate resource to clear up every single one.

Is this some kind of textbook that's going to transform you into a whole-hog cook-off-winning pitmaster? No. But is it going to deliver quick hits of essential info that will make you feel like an absolute boss at the grill? One hundred percent. I am here to give you all the basics—and I do mean basics—that will have you set for a lifetime of grilling seasons. We'll talk about different types of grills, how they work, and how to pick what's right for you. I'll get you geared up with what you actually need, and I'll hold your hand through turning your grill on, keeping it at the right temperature, and cleaning it when you're done. I've collected some of the most frequently asked questions from WGC, and I'll offer up my insight. By the time you're done with the very first chapter of this book, you're going to wonder where the grill has been all your life—and you haven't even gotten to the recipes yet!

Like all the other dishes I've shared with you over the years, these have had to meet the same tough criteria: They need to deliver irresistible, gooey, saucy, crunchy layers of flavors and textures. They need to suit every mood

and season. And, most important, they need to be easy enough for a weeknight but exciting enough for a weekend. And yes, that includes tons of nonmeat options like pizza, nachos, next-level veg dishes like Marinated Grilled Cabbage with Creamy Labneh (page 165) and Grilled Chimi Mushrooms (page 150), and even salads like Grilled Wedge Cobb Salad (page 162). That said, I've also hooked it up with all the seafood, chicken, pork, beef, and lamb preparations that will help make those plain burger days a distant memory, like Crispy Grilled Wings with Calabrian Vinaigrette (page 44), Sausage and Shrimp Paella (page 87), and Korean Short Ribs with Creamy Kimchi Potato Salad (page 32). Plus, I've got you covered for all your cocktail needs because it just wouldn't be right to be grilling empty-handed. And in case you thought just because we're talking about grilling that there wouldn't be desserts, my Snickerdoodle Pizookie (page 174) and Raspberry Galette with Whipped Cream (page 186) most definitely say otherwise.

I don't know about you, but I'm definitely dreaming about a Grilled Lime Mojito (page 214) and a Juicy Lucy (page 127) right now. So go get your gear, grab a recipe or two (or one of my special menus sprinkled throughout the book), and let's light it up!

xoxo Gaby

GRILLING IS A STATE OF MIND, AKA YOU DON'T NECESSARILY NEED A GRILL TO GRILL

I know this might sound a little strange, but you don't actually need a grill in order to enjoy the recipes in this book. They're going to deliver the same quick, easy, delicious results no matter where you cook them because they're teaching you the basics of flavoring food and treating it right with heat. So, if for any reason you are not able to have a grill, or you want to make these recipes in the dead of winter, I want you to know that you're still welcome here. Many of these recipes can easily be adapted to the stovetop and oven, and I'm going to give you the guidance you need to make that happen.

LET'S GET INTO IT

At its heart, grilling isn't much more than heat + time + food—the same equation you use whether you're cooking in the oven, on the stovetop, or in an air fryer. And I want to do everything I can to preserve that simplicity, because that's pretty much all you need to know to yield perfectly delicious results. That said, just like in any other cookbook, the more prepared you are before you cook, whether it's the tools in your kitchen, the ingredients you have stocked, or the tips and tricks you're equipped with, the easier and more enjoyable the experience will be. So that's what this chapter is all about.

GRILLS

Before you start your grilling adventure, you obviously need a grill. Or you need to know a little more about the grill that you have. The biggest differences between the two main types—gas and charcoal—are how you light them and how you sustain the heat you want while you cook. Let's break it down a little more:

GAS GRILL: This is the simplest, easiest type of grill to use and is truly your everyday grilling gadget. It lights just like your gas stovetop, gets hot in seconds, and is zoned so that you can create different levels of heat in different parts of your grill with the turn of a dial.

CHARCOAL GRILL: The major pro of a charcoal grill is that you're getting that classic wood-fire smoke and typically for less money than a gas grill. The downside is that these grills are more involved to light, take longer to heat (about 45 minutes is the rule of thumb), and are not as straightforward in terms of maintaining the level of heat.

SIZE DOESN'T MATTER

Both charcoal and gas grills come in all different shapes and sizes, none of which affects your actual cooking other than how much food you can fit on the grill at one time. What makes this so great is that you can find the perfect grill regardless of whether you're completing a patio setup or kitting out your fire escape. (Safety first, though, please!)

WHAT ABOUT SMOKERS?

People often ask me about smokers: In addition to a grill, they can definitely have a place in your outdoor cooking setup. Between my father and my BFF Adam, there's been a lot of smoking in my life, and both of these guys convinced me how magical that low, slow heat can be for meat and vegetables. It's especially nice for cooking fattier cuts of meat because it allows the fat to slowly render and the meat to retain its moisture. And you can also use it for anything else you want to give that tantalizing kiss of smoke as you are treating it like an oven. But it is a little more limited in terms of the type of cooking

you use it for, so if you're looking to buy just one backyard toy, I recommend starting with a grill. In the meantime, you can use your oven to make any of the smoker recipes in this book. AND, I'll show you how to soup up your grill—gas or charcoal—to get even more smoky flavor.

GEAR

These are the essentials. Invest in these items—none of which is particularly expensive and most of which you can find at your local hardware store—and I guarantee that you'll use them over and over again. Having a grilling station stocked with these simple tools will mean that you'll be able to cook a wider variety of recipes with greater ease and better results, which is what we're all about here.

1. **TONGS:** For flipping and moving items on the grill

2. **DIGITAL THERMOMETER:** For that extra peace of mind that your meats are perfectly cooked

3. **GRILL SCRAPER:** Key for keeping your grill

clean. (I prefer the coil ones or the steam versions.)

4. **OVEN MITTS:** For hot items coming off the grill

5. **GRILLING SPATULA:** These are larger and sturdier than anything you're using on the stove. They're great for moving large items or more than one item at a time.

6. **GRILLING BASKET:** Perfect for keeping smaller items like mushrooms and green beans from falling through the grates. There are also hinged grilling baskets, which make cooking fish and shrimp a breeze.

7. **CAST-IRON SKILLET:** Allows you to use the grill like a cooktop, plus make skillet cakes. Need I say more?

8. **PLANCHA/FLATTOP:** This creates an instant flattop griddle on your grill. I love using it for something like a smash burger or a veg like asparagus so you don't have to worry about it falling through the grates.

9. **PIZZA STONE:** While you don't NEED a pizza stone for any of the recipes in this book, or to grill pizza, if you want one on hand to make your life a little easier, consider adding to your collection.

FOR CHARCOAL GRILLS AND SMOKERS:

10. **BRIQUETTES OR HARDWOOD CHARCOAL OR HARD-WOOD:** Briquettes are those familiar-looking black chunks of charcoal. They're made out of sawdust and scrap wood; because they're not made out of solid wood, they are inexpensive. However, they don't get as hot as hardwood charcoal. If you go this route, make sure to not get the ones that are soaked with starter fluid because it can affect the taste of the food.

Hardwood charcoal is made from oak or other hardwoods such as walnut, mesquite, and cherry, which adds noticeable flavor to your food. Some grocery stores and most hardware stores keep hardwood charcoal in stock.

Hardwood is what hard-core smoker enthusiasts use because it delivers that distinctive smoky flavor. That said, it can take a little longer to get enough heat going for smoking (closer to an hour). See page 20 for a list of great woods to look for and what they pair well with. Absolute no-no's are painted or chemically treated woods.

11. CHARCOAL CHIMNEY: This helps get your charcoal nice and hot. See the Getting Started section below for a tutorial on how to use it.

12. UTILITY LIGHTER: This is the best way to light things from a distance.

13. THERMOMETER GUN: This will help take the guesswork out of what temperature your grill is running at.

GETTING STARTED

I'll reference these steps and tidbits throughout the recipes because they really are at the foundation of grilling. Consider this everything you need to know!

LIGHTING A CHARCOAL GRILL

1. Set your chimney on the grate of your grill. Fill the bottom third of the chamber with crumpled paper (I like newspaper) and add your charcoal on top.

2. Use your utility lighter to light the paper. After 10 to 15 minutes, the flames will ignite the charcoal. And in about 45 minutes, the charcoals will be ready to use.

3. When the charcoals are covered in gray ashes, carefully turn them out into the bottom of your grill in an even layer. A general rule of thumb is that the more closely the charcoals are bunched, the hotter they'll burn, but more on that on page 17. The embers will last about 1 hour.

WHAT ABOUT LIGHTER FLUID?

It smells weird, it's dangerous, it's illegal in some states. Make friends with your chimney and you'll never look back.

SEASONING YOUR GRILL TO PREVENT STICKING

Just like you season a cast-iron pan to prevent sticking, the same goes for a grill. Pro tip: Starting with a clean grill will make this easier. See page 18 for how to leave it cleaner than you found it.

STEP 1: Before turning on the grill, coat the surface of the grate with high-heat cooking oil. I like using half an onion with the cut side slathered in oil—instant flavor and you're not wasting paper towels. That said, you can also douse a paper towel in oil and use that. In both cases, using tongs is handy so you don't get your hands greasy. Canola oil and peanut oil work well, but you could also use coconut oil or a vegetable oil spray.

STEP 2: Wipe any excess oil off the grate with a paper towel, then turn the grill on high for 15 to 20 minutes, until the oil starts to smoke. The grate will start to look darker too.

DIRECT VERSUS INDIRECT HEAT

Direct heat means cooking your food directly

over your source of heat, while indirect heat means cooking it adjacent to your heat source.

With direct-heat cooking on the grill, we're talking about the flames themselves. Direct heat is what's responsible for those gorgeous grill marks, juicy flame-broiled burgers, and crispy vegetables. It's also great for quick-cooking foods like hot dogs and most seafood like shrimp, and for getting that nice golden crust on your proteins.

Indirect heat on the grill is when you have a cooking "zone" that's heated by fire but isn't in direct contact with the flame. Cooking like this is similar to using your oven. Think potatoes wrapped in foil, whole chickens or racks of ribs sitting on the grate with the flames in that zone reduced to low or turned off, and traditional barbecue cooked low and slow in a smoker.

It's possible to use both direct and indirect heat in one preparation—called *combo heat*, if you want to seem like you really know your stuff. Combo heat or combo cooking is most often used with large pieces of meat, which first get seared over direct heat and then are slowly cooked over indirect heat. (Just like searing something in a pan on the stove before transferring it to the oven.) Combo heat is also great for grilling fruit and denser vegetables like carrots and cabbage, so they get that beautiful char before getting nice and tender with less intense heat.

CONTROLLING TEMPERATURE

For gas grills, this is a piece of cake—they have knobs that tell you what level of heat you're getting in each zone.

For charcoal, it's slightly more involved, but not too complicated once you get a feel for it. But first, we need to get a little science-y. Oxygen feeds fire, so the more air your fire is exposed to, the hotter it will be. Charcoal grills have two dampers, which allow air to flow into the grill. If you open those dampers wider, you get a hotter fire. Close them up and the temperature cools. To keep things simple, I recommend keeping the damper at the bottom of your grill open, then using the damper on your lid to control the temperature.

There are a number of factors that affect the temperature of your grill besides air flow (how windy it is outside, how much crud might be left on your grill grates, the food you're grilling), but here's a basic guide for how to affect the temperature with your damper:

HIGH HEAT
(450°F to 500°F/230°C to 260°C): fully open

MEDIUM HEAT
(350°F to 450°F/175°C to 230°C): half open

LOW HEAT
(250°F to 350°F/120°C to 175°C): quarter open

LOW SMOKING HEAT
(225°F to 275°F/110°C to 135°C): quarter to an eighth open

OFF: fully closed

In the beginning, as you're getting used to these temperatures, feel free to use your thermometer gun to give you peace of mind. Your grill will also most likely have a thermometer built into the lid. Be sure to keep the ash catcher of your grill cleaned out (page 20), or it can get in the way of your damper and affect the heat settings.

What does *carryover cooking* mean? Meat will continue cooking even after you've removed it from a heat source (grilling or otherwise). If your steak hits the perfect medium-rare temperature on the grill (which we'll talk more about in a bit), the temperature will continue to rise several degrees while it is resting. On average, the temperature of meat will increase 10 degrees Fahrenheit (5 degrees Celsius) or more during this time, depending on size (the larger the cut, the more carryover cooking occurs). So keep this in mind when deciding the cook time for your preferred level of doneness. The sweet spot is 5 to 10 degrees Fahrenheit (3 to 5 degrees Celsius) below your desired doneness. And if you're still concerned about nailing the right temp, that's when your thermometer comes into play.

AT-A-GLANCE TEMPS FOR DONENESS

No more doneness mysteries! Use this handy chart to determine what your ideal temp is when cooking meat. Don't forget about carryover cooking (page 17)!

BEEF	LAMB	POULTRY	PORK
RARE 120°F to 125°F (48.9°C to 51.5°C)	**RARE** 135°F (57°C)	**CHICKEN** 165°F to 175°F (74°C to 80°C)	**MEDIUM-RARE** 145°F to 150°F (63°C to 65.5°C)
MEDIUM-RARE 130°F to 135°F (54.4°C to 57°C)	**MEDIUM-RARE** 140°F to 150°F (60°C to 65.5°C)	**TURKEY** 165°F to 175°F (74°C to 80°C)	**MEDIUM** 150°F to 155°F (65.5°C to 68.5°C)
MEDIUM 140°F to 145°F (60°C to 63°C)	**MEDIUM** 160°F (71°C)		**MEDIUM-WELL** 155°F to 160°F (68.5°C to 71°C)
MEDIUM-WELL 150°F to 155°F (65.5°C to 68.5°C)	**MEDIUM-WELL** 150°F to 155°F (65.5°C to 68.5°C)		**WELL DONE** 160°F (71°C)
WELL DONE 160°F (71°C) and above	**WELL DONE** 165°F (74°C) and above		

CLOSING UP SHOP

After each use, when the grill has had a few minutes of burn time after the food comes off, use a wire brush to scrape off any accumulated bits from the grates. Then, before you even serve dinner or sit down to eat, turn off the grill.

Take it from someone who may or may not have forgotten to turn off the grill a few times while working as a private chef: Do it while it's fresh in your mind. When the grill cools, apply a thin coat of high-heat cooking oil.

For gas grills, simply turn the knobs to "off" and close the valve on the gas tank. For charcoal grills, close the air vents on the side of the grill and cover with the lid.

ONE LAST STEP FOR CHARCOAL GRILLS: Be sure to not let too much ash accumulate in the drum of the grill, or it could affect how much air gets into the damper. Follow the manufacturer's instructions for removing the base of the grill, then collect the (cooled!) ashes in aluminum foil or a metal container with a lid to ensure that there's zero fire risk when you throw them away.

EXTRA CREDIT: FLAVORING YOUR SMOKE

Whether you're using a smoker, charcoal grill, or gas grill, you can use hardwood—whole logs or wood chips—to change up the flavor of your food.

For charcoal grills, you can set the wood in a crisscross pattern directly over your embers, then use a utility lighter to light them. After about 1 hour, they should be smoldering and ready to spread over the bottom of your grill. (You can use your thermometer gun to determine whether they're hot enough.)

For gas grills, purchase a smoker box, which is pretty much what it sounds like—a small stainless-steel box that sits on your grill grates and gets everything nice and smoky.

THE MOST AROMATIC WOODS TO USE ARE:
   HICKORY: Synonymous with barbecue. It's got that baconlike flavor and is perfect with ribs and red meat.

   PECAN: Fruity and pungent, so use an easy hand with this one. It does burn cooler, though, which makes it great for larger cuts that need the low, slow treatment.

ALDER: More delicate and naturally sweet, which makes it well suited for fish, poultry, pork, and lighter meats.

APPLE: Mild and slightly fruity. It's usually what's used to smoke ham and would also be nice with fish and poultry.

CHERRY: Also mild and fruity and will turn whatever you're cooking a deep mahogany color. It's great with beef and pork, but best used as part of a blend with hickory, oak, pecan, or alder.

GRAPEVINE CUTTINGS: I know, I know, but in case you come by some, they produce a mild smoke that's good with lighter proteins like fish, poultry, and some beef like skirt and flank steaks.

MESQUITE: Bold and slightly sweet, and also best used in combination with another wood. It burns hot and fast, so stick to smaller cuts that don't require prolonged cooking time.

OAK: The just-right medium. It's smokier than cherry or apple but milder than hickory and mesquite. It's great with red meat, pork, and game. You can usually find white or red oak; you'll get a little more mileage out of red.

GETTING YOUR TIMING RIGHT

Grilling is truly one of the quickest and easiest ways to cook something, but in order to get the best results, there's often some prep that needs to be done first. To make sure that you don't end up crunched for time when you're ready to cook, leave yourself enough time for these crucial steps:

1. BRINING OR MARINATING YOUR MEAT OR VEG: This is where the flavor starts to happen because it allows seasonings to seep directly into the food and is also the equivalent of sautéing with oil or butter to ensure your ingredients take heat well and don't dry out. In a pinch you can get away with a quick dip, but if you think you'll be short on time, get marinating the night before so everything gets a nice long soak and you won't have to deal with this bit when you're trying to throw together dinner.

2. **LETTING YOUR MEAT COME UP TO TEMP**: I like to let meat come to room temperature for 30 minutes before throwing it on the grill. Taking the chill off your meat will help it cook more evenly and will ensure that you don't have to cook it longer than necessary, which keeps it juicier.

3. **LETTING YOUR MEAT REST:** Don't slice into your meat the second it comes off the grill! You want to give it at least a few minutes for the carryover cooking to run its course and, most important, for the juices to redistribute. Otherwise all that juicy goodness will go running out onto your cutting board instead of getting soaked back up into the meat. A good rule of thumb is to let it rest for about half the time it cooks. If cooked low and slow, let it rest for 10 to 15 minutes for the juices to redistribute.

BUYING MEAT

A huge cost-saver is being your own butcher. That means buying larger cuts of meat and cutting them into portions at home. You can cut down a 10-pound (4.5 kg) rib eye roast into steaks, a tenderloin into filets, a whole pork loin into chops, or a whole chicken into parts. Then pack those pieces in an airtight zip-top bag (squeezing out as much air as possible so the meat doesn't oxidize) and stash them in the freezer so you'll be able to meal plan and prep at a moment's notice.

LET'S TALK ABOUT FAT

Bottom line: Fat is flavor. So the more fat a cut of meat has, no matter what kind of meat, the juicier and more flavorful it will be. Fattier cuts of steak like rib eye, T-bone, and New York strip usually have a fat cap, or thick strip of fat running along the edge of the steak. When it comes to grilling, you can get even more mileage out of that fat. The easiest thing to do is to leave the fat on and allow it to naturally baste the meat as it cooks. Another option is to trim off the fat cap and use it a couple of different ways. With a pair of tongs, you can run it over a preheated grill as a nonstick spray alternative. Or, if you're feeling adventurous, you could grind up the fat and add it to burgers and sausages.

BEEF.

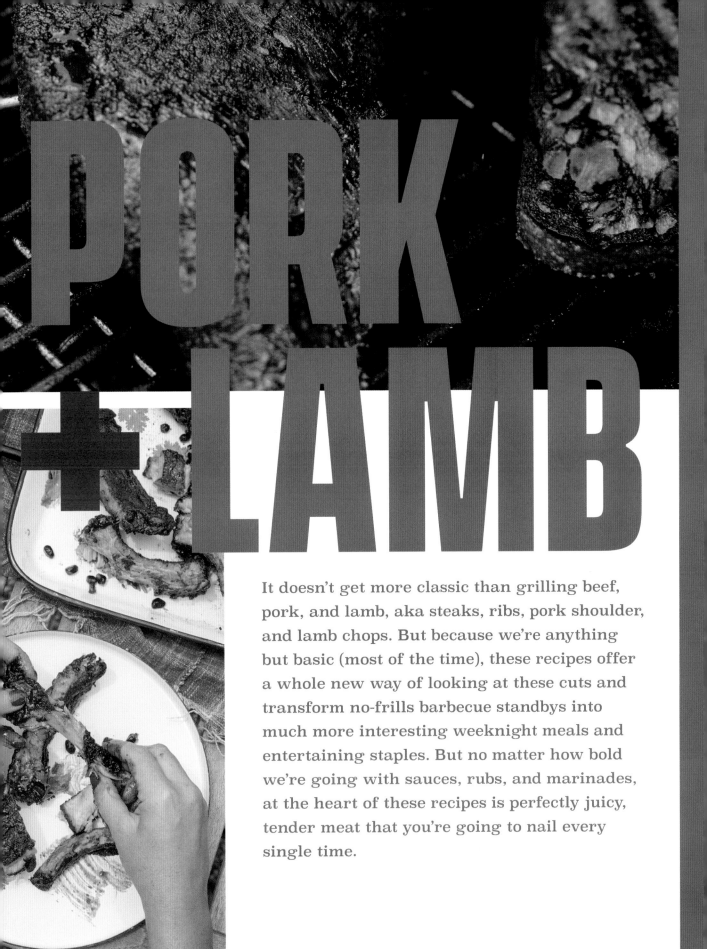

PORK + LAMB

It doesn't get more classic than grilling beef, pork, and lamb, aka steaks, ribs, pork shoulder, and lamb chops. But because we're anything but basic (most of the time), these recipes offer a whole new way of looking at these cuts and transform no-frills barbecue standbys into much more interesting weeknight meals and entertaining staples. But no matter how bold we're going with sauces, rubs, and marinades, at the heart of these recipes is perfectly juicy, tender meat that you're going to nail every single time.

The One and Only
STEAK RECIPE

PREP TIME: 5 minutes (spice rub version) or 2 to 8 hours (marinade version)   **COOK TIME:** 10 minutes
YIELD: Serves 3 or 4

One of my favorite ways to cook steak is on the grill, namely because it's ideal for getting that perfect crust on the outside, which locks in all the juiciness on the inside. So I wanted to come up with a recipe that will work for any kind of cut that you buy or have on hand. Go with my favorite hanger steak, Adam's favorite rib eye, or you do you! You also get to choose between a rub and a marinade, which comes down to personal preference too. I love both of these vehicles for flavor, and both have a place in my kitchen. Marinades are great if you have time and can come in handy if you're using a tougher cut of meat that could use some tenderizing (think skirt steak, hanger steak, and flank steak). Rubs, on the other hand, are nice and quick. Just don't go for both at the same time or it'll be seasoning overload.

FOR THE SPICE RUB VERSION:

2 tablespoons freshly cracked black pepper

2 tablespoons freshly cracked white pepper

1 tablespoon cayenne pepper

1 tablespoon granulated onion

¼ cup (42 g) granulated garlic

¼ cup (34 g) Diamond Crystal kosher salt

FOR THE MARINADE VERSION:

4 green onions, white and light green parts only, sliced super thin

4 cloves garlic, finely chopped

⅓ cup (70 ml) reduced-sodium soy sauce

2 tablespoons fresh lime juice

1 tablespoon olive oil

1 teaspoon red pepper flakes

Kosher salt and freshly cracked black pepper

FOR THE STEAK:

2 (1- to 1½-pound/455 to 680 g) hanger steaks (or other steak of your preference)

Flaky sea salt

FOR THE SPICE RUB VERSION: Place all the seasonings in a bowl and stir to combine. Use 3 to 4 tablespoons of the rub to coat both sides of the steak (store the rest of the rub in an airtight container for another time). Spice rub will keep for for roughly 12 months, but I guarantee you will use it faster than that!

FOR THE MARINADE VERSION: Put all the ingredients for the marinade in a medium bowl and whisk to combine. Place the steaks in a zip-top bag, add the marinade, and zip closed, removing excess air. Make sure the marinade is coating all sides of the steak and let marinate in the fridge for at least 2 hours and up to 8 hours.

TO GRILL THE STEAK: Heat a gas or charcoal grill to medium-high heat (400°F to 450°F/205°C to 230°C) and lightly oil the grates.

For the marinade version, remove the steak from the marinade and let it come to room temperature for 30 minutes. Season with salt and pepper. For both versions, grill the steaks for 4 to 5 minutes per side for medium-rare. Remove from the grill. Let rest for 5 to 10 minutes, then slice against the grain. Sprinkle with sea salt and serve.

Zack's Brined
PORK CHOPS

PREP TIME: 10 minutes **MARINATING TIME:** 4 to 24 hours **COOK TIME:** 12 minutes **YIELD:** Serves 4

In addition to being one of my best friends, the husband to my very best friend, the officiant of my wedding, and a total cocktail genius (who helped curate the drinks chapter in this book), Zack introduced me to this pork chop recipe to end all pork chop recipes. By letting the chops marinate overnight in a brown sugar, garlic, and fresh herb-infused brine, they soak up all that tasty flavor and maintain even more moisture as they cook. After getting smoky and caramelized on the grill, they're the perfect canvas for just about any topping or sauce from pages 224–233.

Combine the water, salt, brown sugar, rosemary, thyme, sage, bay leaf, peppercorns, and garlic in a medium saucepan. Bring to a simmer over medium heat and simmer for 10 minutes. Turn the heat off.

Add 2 cups (240 g) ice and melt to bring to room temperature. Place the pork chops in a large zip-top bag and pour in the liquid. Zip closed, removing excess air.

Transfer to the fridge and let brine for at least 4 hours or up to 24 hours if possible.

Once you're ready to grill, remove the pork chops from the brine, pat dry, and season liberally with salt and pepper.

Heat a gas or charcoal grill to medium-high heat (400°F to 450°F/205°C to 230°C) and lightly oil the grates. Grill the pork chops for 5 to 6 minutes per side, until grill marks appear and the internal temp of the pork is 145°F (63°C). Let rest for 10 minutes and serve.

2 cups (480 ml) water

¼ cup (34 g) Diamond Crystal kosher salt, plus more for seasoning the pork chops

2 to 3 tablespoons light brown sugar

1 fresh rosemary sprig

2 fresh thyme sprigs

1 small bunch fresh sage

1 bay leaf

1 tablespoon black peppercorns

4 cloves garlic, smashed

4 (10- to 12-ounce/280 to 340 g) bone-in pork chops

Freshly cracked black pepper

A NOTE FROM ZACK: "I like using Santa Maria seasoning for Cali vibes, but salt and pepper is all you need."

The perfect
CARNE ASADA

PREP TIME: 10 minutes   **MARINATING TIME:** 4 to 5 hours   **COOK TIME:** 10 minutes   **YIELD:** Serves 6 to 8

The name says it all, people! You know that I am all about that taco life, and you can't have tacos without carne asada, or skirt steak that's been slathered in a jalapeño, garlic, and cilantro-spiked marinade. And you know that also means salsa and guac, because obviously. This is the kind of recipe you could make for an easy weeknight meal or scale up for a crowd-pleasing feast that doesn't break the bank.

6 cloves garlic, roughly chopped

1 jalapeño chile, roughly chopped

1 cup (60 g) roughly chopped
   fresh cilantro

Juice of 2 limes

Juice of 1 orange

½ cup (120 ml) olive oil

Kosher salt and freshly cracked
   black pepper

2 pounds (910 g) skirt steak

Charred corn or flour tortillas

Pico de Gallo (page 228)

Guacamole (page 228)

Combine the garlic, jalapeño, cilantro, lime juice, orange juice, and oil in a blender and blend until smooth. Remove, taste, and season with salt and pepper as needed. Reserve ¼ cup (60 ml) of the marinade. Place the steak in a large baking dish and cover with the remaining marinade. Cover with plastic wrap and refrigerate for 4 to 5 hours.

Heat a gas or charcoal grill to high heat (450°F to 500°F/230°C to 260°C) and lightly oil the grates. Grill the steak for about 5 minutes on each side, until done to your liking. Remove from the grill and brush with the remaining marinade. Let rest for 5 to 10 minutes, then slice against the grain. Serve with tortillas, pico de gallo, and guacamole.

Smoked
PORK SHOULDER

PREP TIME: 5 minutes   **MARINATING TIME:** 12 to 24 hours   **COOK TIME:** 7 to 10 hours   **YIELD:** Serves 8

About seven years ago I was introduced to the wonder that is the smoker. To me, it's the ultimate set-it-and-forget-it tool because it's meant to cook things at a relatively low temperature for a longer period of time. The result is smoke-infused, melt-in-your mouth meat, which is perfectly suited for a bigger cut like pork shoulder. After you let the smoker (or oven) do its thing—which is almost completely hands-off time—all you need to do is toss the meat with some BBQ sauce and pile it high on a brioche bun, a baked potato, or freshly baked corn bread.

Trim excess fat from the pork shoulder, but make sure to leave a layer of fat on top. With a sharp knife, score the fat cap in a diamond pattern (don't cut into the meat).

Combine the sugar and salt in a small bowl and rub the mixture all over the shoulder. Place in a baking pan, cover loosely with plastic wrap, and refrigerate for at least 12 hours or up to 24 hours.

Remove the pork shoulder from the refrigerator and scrape any remaining sugar and salt off the shoulder. Sprinkle on the BBQ rub and rub it in with your hands. Let sit at room temp for 30 minutes.

Meanwhile, preheat a pellet smoker to 250°F (120°C), load the hopper with wood pellets (apple pellets work well with pork), and let it heat up with the lid closed for at least 15 minutes. (If you are using an oven, preheat to 250°F/120°C.)

Place the pork directly on the grill grates, fat-side up, and cook until the internal temperature reaches 160°F (71°C), 4 to 5 hours. (If you are using an oven, bake the pork until the internal temperature reaches 160°F/71°C, 4 to 5 hours.)

Remove the pork from the smoker and place in an aluminum roasting pan. Pour the apple juice over the pork and cover tightly with foil. Return to the smoker and continue to cook until the internal temperature reaches 205°F (96°C), 3 to 5 hours longer. (If you are using an oven, follow the same process and return the pork with apple juice to the smoker for another 3 to 5 hours.)

Remove from the smoker and let rest, covered, for 30 to 45 minutes.

Carefully remove the liquid from the pan and separate out as much fat as you can. Reserve the pan juices. Shred or chop the pork into your desired size, removing and discarding the bone and any excess fat. Toss in BBQ sauce and the reserved pan juices and serve on soft hamburger buns, baked potatoes, or corn bread with your desired toppings.

NOTE: If you have any leftovers, toss 'em in a hot cast-iron skillet to crisp them up and make carnitas!

1 (6- to 9-pound/2.7 to 4 kg) bone-in pork shoulder

1 cup (200 g) granulated sugar

½ cup (68 g) Diamond Crystal kosher salt

¼ cup (60 ml) your favorite BBQ spice rub

1½ cups (360 ml) apple juice

BBQ sauce

Soft hamburger buns, baked potatoes, or freshly baked corn bread

TOPPINGS:
Pickled Red Onions (page 226)
Pickled or fresh sliced jalapeños
Super Creamy Coleslaw with a Kick (page 136)

Korean
SHORT RIBS with Creamy Kimchi Potato Salad

PREP TIME: 15 minutes **MARINATING TIME:** 4 to 24 hours **COOK TIME:** 8 minutes **YIELD:** Serves 6 to 8

The What's Gaby Cooking team is a well-oiled machine, largely because we all share a love of good food and good times while we cook, photograph, and, of course, eat the fruits of our labor. One of our key players is Diana Kim, a food styling goddess who not only makes these dishes look gorgeous but also brings the most incredible traditional Korean preparations to the set. Anyone who has checked out the Korean Dinner Party on whatsgabycooking.com knows her handiwork, and these sweet-smoky short ribs plus a fun kimchi and potato salad mash-up is another one for the record books.

FOR THE MARINADE:

1 medium white onion, roughly chopped

10 cloves garlic, peeled

1 small Asian pear, peeled, cored, and roughly chopped (can sub Bartlett pear or Pink Lady apple)

1 (1- to 2-inch/2.5 to 5 cm) piece fresh ginger, peeled and roughly chopped

3 green onions, white and light green parts only, roughly chopped

¼ cup (60 ml) water

⅓ cup (70 ml) reduced-sodium soy sauce

⅓ cup (60 g) dark brown sugar

⅓ cup (70 ml) rice wine or white wine

1 tablespoon toasted sesame oil

2½ teaspoons freshly cracked black pepper

½ teaspoon Korean chile powder or cayenne pepper

FOR THE RIBS:

5 pounds (2.3 kg) bone-in, flanken-style Korean short ribs

4 green onions, white and light green parts only, thinly sliced on the bias

Creamy Kimchi Potato Salad (page 232)

TO MAKE THE MARINADE: Combine all the ingredients in a blender and blend until smooth. Set aside until ready to use. This makes about 4 cups (960 ml); you can freeze any extra for another use.

TO MAKE THE RIBS: Place the ribs into an XL or 2-gallon (2.5 L) zip-top bag, pour in the marinade, and zip closed, removing as much air as possible. Refrigerate for at least 4 hours and up to 24 hours.

Heat a gas or charcoal grill to medium-high heat (400°F to 450°F/205°C to 230°C) and lightly oil the grates.

Remove the ribs from the marinade, draining off excess. Grill the short ribs, turning once, to desired doneness, 3 to 4 minutes per side. Let rest for 5 to 7 minutes.

Serve whole as a main course or cut into smaller pieces using kitchen shears for an appetizer. Garnish with thinly sliced green onions and serve with the creamy kimchi potato salad.

Smoked
BABY BACK RIBS with Chipotle Pomegranate BBQ Sauce

PREP TIME: 30 minutes   **MARINATING TIME:** 1 to 24 hours   **COOK TIME:** 4 hours   **YIELD:** Serves 4 to 6

I live for ribs. They are the quintessential summer recipe for me, namely because nothing says super-casual outdoor entertaining like everyone getting elbow-deep in BBQ sauce as they take these down to the bone. I learned my technique from the very best: my Grandma Sandy. She was the family's original rib aficionado, and she taught me the importance of leaving no meat behind. So I dedicate this revamped recipe—complete with a sticky, tangy sauce—to her. I like to use cherry, apple, or pecan wood pellets for a sweet smoke flavor. This recipe is best for pellet smokers, which can get hotter than stand-alone smokers.

Place the sugar, paprika, salt, pepper, onion, garlic, ginger, coriander, and cinnamon in a bowl and mix to combine.

Brush the ribs with the mustard, then evenly sprinkle the rub on all sides of the ribs. Cover and let sit in the refrigerator for at least 1 hour and up to 24 hours.

When ready to cook, preheat a pellet smoker to 250°F (120°C), load the hopper with wood pellets, and let it heat up with the lid closed for at least 15 minutes. (Follow the manufacturer's instructions for smoker start-up.) Remove the ribs from the refrigerator and place a digital thermometer into one of the ribs in the thickest part of the meat, making sure to not touch any bones. Place the ribs on the smoker bone-side down and close the lid.

After 2 hours, transfer the apple juice to a spray bottle (if you don't have a spray bottle, you can mop the juice on with a brush). Give the ribs a spray and repeat the spray every 30 minutes until the internal temperature of the ribs hits 205°F (95°C) and the ribs are browned and feel tender, about 2 hours more.

Remove the ribs from the smoker, place on a baking sheet, and slather chipotle pomegranate BBQ sauce on all sides.

Increase the temperature of the smoker to 400°F (204°C). Once the smoker comes up to temperature, place the sauced ribs onto the grill meat-side down. Smoke for 6 to 8 minutes per side, until the sauce looks set.

Remove from the grill and cut into half racks or individual ribs. Garnish with pomegranate arils and cilantro and serve with more BBQ sauce on the side.

¼ cup (50 g) dark brown sugar

¼ cup (25 g) smoked paprika

2 tablespoons kosher salt

2 tablespoons freshly ground black pepper

1 tablespoon granulated onion

1 tablespoon granulated garlic

1 teaspoon ground ginger

1 teaspoon ground coriander

½ teaspoon ground cinnamon

4 (2- to 2½-pound/910 g to 1.2 kg) racks baby back ribs, membrane removed

2 tablespoons yellow mustard

2 cups (480 ml) apple juice

Chipotle Pomegranate BBQ Sauce (recipe follows)

Pomegranate arils, for garnish

Fresh cilantro, for garnish

(recipe continues)

CHIPOTLE POMEGRANATE BBQ SAUCE

PREP TIME: 10 minutes
COOK TIME: 30 minutes
YIELD: Makes about 2½ cups (540 ml)

1 tablespoon olive oil
½ red onion, finely chopped
2 cloves garlic, chopped
Kosher salt and freshly ground black pepper
1 cup (240 ml) ketchup
½ cup (120 ml) pomegranate molasses

2 to 3 chipotle chiles in adobo
¼ cup (50 g) light brown sugar
2 tablespoons apple cider vinegar
1½ teaspoons Worcestershire sauce
1 tablespoon dry mustard
1 teaspoon ground cumin
1 teaspoon paprika

Heat the oil in a large saucepan over medium heat. Add the onion and garlic and season with salt and pepper. Cook for 5 minutes, or until the onion is softened. Add the ketchup, molasses, chipotles, brown sugar, vinegar, Worcestershire sauce, dry mustard, cumin, and paprika. Season with salt and pepper again and stir to combine.

Blend with an immersion blender (or move the sauce to a standing blender) until smooth. Bring to a simmer, then reduce the heat to low and cook for 15 to 20 minutes, until thickened up enough to coat the back of a spoon. Transfer to a container and cool to room temperature. The sauce will keep, covered and refrigerated, for up to 2 weeks.

Smoked Spiced
TRI-TIP with Calabrian Chimichurri

PREP TIME: 10 minutes   **MARINATING TIME:** 20 minutes   **COOK TIME:** 30 minutes   **YIELD:** Serves 6

As you most likely know by now, we California girls—in geography and in spirit—are obsessed with all things tri-tip. It's a popular cut of meat here, particularly in the central and southern regions, where it's often cooked over an open flame or grilled. It's also a great cut for smoking and roasting, so the bottom line is that this book would not be complete without a recipe for it. It's such a flavorful cut that you don't want to do anything to get in its way other than give it just the right amount of char and slather it with this Calabrian chile chimi. Dinner—for two, for four, for a crowd—is served. For this recipe, any wood will do, but mesquite, hickory, and oak are particularly good choices.

FOR THE TRI-TIP SPICE RUB AND ROAST:

2 tablespoons light brown sugar

1 tablespoon chipotle chile powder

1 tablespoon paprika

2 teaspoons kosher salt

2 teaspoons freshly ground
  black pepper

1 teaspoon cayenne pepper

1 teaspoon garlic powder

1 teaspoon ground coriander

½ teaspoon ground cumin

3 pounds (1.4 kg) tri-tip roast

FOR THE CALABRIAN CHILE CHIMICHURRI:

3 cloves garlic, finely minced

½ cup (50 g) finely chopped
  fresh parsley

½ cup (50 g) finely chopped
  fresh cilantro

1 tablespoon dried oregano

2 tablespoons roughly chopped
  Calabrian chiles

2 tablespoons red wine vinegar

1 tablespoon honey

¼ cup (60 ml) olive oil

Salt and freshly ground black pepper

TO MAKE THE SPICE RUB AND COOK THE MEAT: Place all the spices in a small bowl and stir to combine. Trim excess fat off the tri-tip and place on a tray. Coat all over with the rub and let rest on the counter for 20 minutes. While the meat is resting, preheat a pellet smoker to 375°F (190°C), load the hopper with wood pellets, and let it heat up with the lid closed for at least 15 minutes.

Place the tri-tip on the grill grates and cook for 30 minutes, flipping halfway through, until the internal temperature registers 135°F (57°C). Place on a cutting board and let rest for 15 minutes, then slice against the grain.

TO MAKE THE CHIMICHURRI: While the tri-tip is cooking, place all the chimichurri ingredients in a medium bowl and stir to combine. Taste and adjust the seasoning if needed. Transfer the chimichurri to a bowl and serve over the tri-tip.

NOTE: Make sure to slice against the grain—this is very important!

LAMB CHOPS with Mint Sauce

PREP TIME: 10 minutes   **MARINATING TIME:** 30 minutes   **COOK TIME:** 4 minutes   **YIELD:** Serves 4 to 5

These are not your mama's prim and proper Easter lamb chops. They're a little louder than polite with tons of fresh herb flavor and smoke plus a punchy mint sauce that runs circles around anything from a jar.

TO MARINATE THE LAMB CHOPS: Place the oil, mustard, lemon zest, garlic, rosemary, thyme, oregano, salt, and pepper in a large bowl and whisk to combine. Add the lamb chops and gently toss to coat all over. Let the lamb chops marinate at room temperature for 30 minutes. (You can also cover and refrigerate for up to 6 hours. Remove from the fridge 30 minutes before grilling.)

Heat a gas or charcoal grill to medium-high heat (400°F to 450°F/205°C to 230°C) and lightly oil the grates.

TO MAKE THE MINT SAUCE: While the lamb is marinating and the grill is coming up to temperature, finely chop the mint, removing any stems, and place in a nonreactive bowl. Add the sugar and boiling water and stir to combine. Add the vinegar and salt and stir to combine again. Set aside until ready to serve.

Remove the lamb chops from the marinade, draining off excess. Put the lamb chops on the grill and cook for 2 minutes per side, or until they register 145°F (63°C) for medium-rare or 160°F (71°C) for medium.

Remove the lamb chops from the grill, drizzle with the mint sauce, and serve.

FOR THE LAMB CHOPS:

⅓ cup (70 ml) olive oil

1 tablespoon Dijon mustard

Zest of 1 lemon

5 cloves garlic, chopped

1 tablespoon chopped fresh rosemary

2 teaspoons chopped fresh thyme leaves

2 teaspoons chopped fresh oregano

2 teaspoons kosher salt

1 teaspoon freshly ground black pepper

2 pounds (910 g) lamb chops (8 to 10 chops), cut ¾ inch (1.9 cm) thick

FOR THE MINT SAUCE:

1 cup (35 g) tightly packed fresh mint leaves

2 teaspoons granulated sugar

¼ cup (60 ml) boiling water

2 tablespoons red wine vinegar

¼ teaspoon kosher salt

CHICKEN

No matter what kind of cooking you're doing, chicken is the ultimate blank canvas. But when you're grilling and transforming that otherwise—let's be honest—ho-hum meat into the most tender, juicy version of itself, adding layers of flavor with rubs, marinades, and sauces takes this inexpensive utility protein from a have-to to a must-have. And we've got no shortage of inspiration to pull from because we'll be traveling around the world, getting pumped about big, bold flavors, from Turkish shawarma to Mexican chipotle-lime to Indonesian satay. It's the kind of glow-up that will have you rethinking everything you know about chicken.

Crispy
GRILLED WINGS
with Calabrian Vinaigrette

PREP TIME: 10 minutes   **COOK TIME:** 20 minutes   **YIELD:** Serves 4 to 6

I feel the same way about wings that I do about ribs: You can never have enough. It's not a party unless everyone's face is covered in sauce, and you have to polish off every last bit of meat or I might reconsider our friendship. And when it comes to my favorite ways to cook them, the grill is at the top of that list. No more messing around with oil splatters for perfectly crispy, flavorful wings. Add this all-purpose spicy Calabrian vinaigrette for dunking, and you have yourself a cookout.

FOR THE CALABRIAN VINAIGRETTE:

3 cloves garlic, roughly chopped

½ cup (30 g) chopped fresh flat-leaf parsley

½ cup (30 g) chopped fresh cilantro

2 tablespoons fresh oregano leaves

2 tablespoons roughly chopped Calabrian chiles

2 tablespoons red wine vinegar

1 tablespoon honey

¼ cup (60 ml) olive oil

Kosher salt and freshly ground black pepper to taste

FOR THE CHICKEN WINGS:

1 tablespoon kosher salt

1 teaspoon freshly ground black pepper

1 teaspoon garlic powder

3 pounds (1.4 kg) whole chicken wings

6 tablespoons unsalted butter

2 tablespoons honey

Preheat a gas or charcoal grill to medium heat (350°F to 400°F/175°C to 204°C) and lightly oil the grates.

TO MAKE THE CALABRIAN VINAIGRETTE: Place all the ingredients in a blender or food processor and pulse until the ingredients are well combined and broken down. Taste and adjust the seasoning if needed. Reserve ⅓ cup (70 ml) for the sauce and refrigerate the rest for up to 1 week or freeze for a few months.

TO GRILL THE WINGS: Combine the salt, pepper, and garlic powder in a small bowl. Place the wings in a large bowl and toss with the salt mixture to evenly coat.

Place the wings on the grill, crowding them together so that they are all touching (this goes against the conventional wisdom of giving meat room so it doesn't steam; but you want them to steam so they stay moist). Grill, flipping the wings every 5 minutes, for a total of 20 minutes.

Meanwhile, combine the butter, the reserved ⅓ cup (70 ml) vinaigrette, and the honey in a saucepan over low heat and whisk until the garlic is fragrant and the butter is melted, 2 to 3 minutes.

Toss the wings with the sauce in a large clean bowl. Turn the heat on the grill up to medium-high (400°F to 450°F/205°C to 230°C). Use tongs to remove the wings from the sauce and place back on the grill. Cook until the skin crisps, 1 to 2 minutes per side. Put the wings back in the bowl, toss, and serve.

Basic B Grilled
CHICKEN SALAD with BBQ Sauce Vinaigrette

PREP TIME: 30 minutes **MARINATING TIME:** 2 to 24 hours **COOK TIME:** 12 minutes **YIELD:** Serves 4

Listen, I know we love our boneless, skinless chicken breasts. They're lean, they deliver the protein you need, they're easy to make . . . blah blah blah. But they are also boring AF unless you really lean in to the seasoning game! You can still get all the health benefits of chicken breast if it's packed with flavor, which marinating it with spices and throwing it on the grill is most certainly going to do. And while we are taking things up a notch, we might as well toss these bad girls in a big-ass chopped salad with a (completely genius) BBQ sauce vinaigrette.

TO MARINATE THE CHICKEN: Place the oil, brown sugar, chili powder, garlic powder, onion powder, cumin, smoked paprika, salt, and pepper in a small bowl and stir to combine. Place the chicken in a large zip-top bag and add the marinade. Zip closed, removing excess air, and mix the chicken into the marinade. Place in the fridge and let it marinate for at least 2 hours or up to 24 hours.

Heat a gas or charcoal grill to medium-high heat (400°F to 450°F/205°C to 230°C) and lightly oil the grates.

Remove the chicken from the marinade, draining off excess. Grill for 5 to 6 minutes per side, until the chicken is cooked through. Remove from the grill and let the chicken rest for 10 minutes. Chop the chicken into bite-size pieces and set aside.

TO MAKE THE CHOPPED SALAD: While the chicken is resting, make the BBQ sauce vinaigrette.

Combine the lettuces, tomatoes, jicama, beans, corn, cucumbers, red onion, pumpkin seeds, crushed tortilla chips, and chicken in a clean large bowl. Drizzle with the BBQ sauce vinaigrette and toss to combine. Sprinkle on the cheese and serve with additional vinaigrette.

FOR THE CHICKEN:
1 tablespoon olive oil

1 tablespoon light brown sugar

1 teaspoon chili powder

1 teaspoon garlic powder

1 teaspoon onion powder

1 teaspoon ground cumin

1 teaspoon smoked paprika

1½ teaspoons kosher salt

1 teaspoon freshly ground black pepper

2 (6- to 8-ounce/170 to 225 g) boneless, skinless chicken breasts

FOR THE CHOPPED SALAD:
BBQ Sauce Vinaigrette (page 230)

4 cups (55 g) chopped romaine lettuce

4 cups (72 g) chopped iceberg lettuce

2 cups (200 g) cherry tomatoes, cut in half

1 cup (130 g) peeled and diced (½-inch/1.25 cm pieces) jicama

1 cup (170 g) canned cannellini beans

1 cup (164 g) fresh corn kernels

2 Persian cucumbers, chopped

½ medium red onion, chopped (about ⅓ cup/55 g)

½ cup (120 g) toasted pumpkin seeds

1 cup (67 g) crushed corn tortilla chips

¾ cup (150 g) crumbled goat cheese or feta cheese

Grilled Cumin
CHICKEN KEBABS

PREP TIME: 15 minutes   **MARINATING TIME:** 1 to 4 hours   **COOK TIME:** 12 minutes   **YIELD:** Serves 6 to 8

I couldn't write a book about grilling and not give you the ultimate kebab recipe. I love a kebab because the smaller bits of meat cook super quickly, and they're easy to load up with tons of flavor—in this case with a spiced marinade that would be perfect no matter what cut or preparation of chicken you're making. But if we're being honest, it's mainly because they're a vehicle for cool, creamy tzatziki, and it would only be right to wrap that all up in soft, doughy pita.

SPECIAL EQUIPMENT:
6 to 8 metal or wooden skewers

1 tablespoon ground cumin

1½ teaspoons granulated garlic

1½ teaspoons paprika

½ teaspoon red pepper flakes

3 tablespoons olive oil

2 tablespoons red wine vinegar

1 teaspoon kosher salt

1 teaspoon freshly ground
   black pepper

6 cloves garlic, roughly chopped

Juice of 1 lemon

3 pounds (1.4 kg) boneless, skinless
   chicken thighs and/or breasts,
   cut into 1¼-inch (3 cm) cubes

Tzatziki (page 228), for serving

1 lemon, halved, lightly oiled, and
   grilled cut-side down until charred,
   for serving

Store-bought pita bread, grilled until
   light grill marks appear, for serving

Chopped fresh dill, for serving

Place the cumin, granulated garlic, paprika, red pepper flakes, oil, vinegar, salt, pepper, garlic, and lemon juice in a large bowl and whisk to combine. Add the chicken and toss to coat. Cover and refrigerate for at least 1 hour or up to 4 hours.

Preheat a gas or charcoal grill to medium-high heat (400°F to 450°F/205°C to 230°C) and lightly oil the grates.

Thread the chicken pieces onto the skewers, dividing them equally. Discard the marinade in the bowl.

Grill the chicken for 10 to 15 minutes, until golden brown and cooked through, turning the skewers occasionally. Transfer the skewers to a platter. Serve with tzatziki, grilled lemon halves, grilled pita bread, and dill.

PRO TIP: If using wooden skewers, be sure to soak them in water for at least 30 minutes before use.

Grilled CHICKEN with Grapes

PREP TIME: 10 minutes **MARINATING TIME:** 1 hour **COOK TIME:** 10 minutes **YIELD:** Serves 4 to 6

OK, I know what you're thinking—grilled grapes? But after five cookbooks and two thousand–plus recipes that I've shared with you, can we agree that I've never steered you wrong? So trust me on this; the grapes get caramelized and deeply sweet, which complements the chicken to a T. It's the meal equivalent of sitting in Sonoma among the vines and sipping a glass of chilled wine.

Place ⅓ cup (70 ml) of the oil, the lemon zest, garlic, mustard, oregano, 1 teaspoon kosher salt, and ½ teaspoon black pepper in a large bowl and whisk to combine. Add the chicken breasts to the mixture and gently toss to coat. Cover the bowl with plastic wrap and let marinate in the fridge for 1 hour.

Preheat a gas or charcoal grill to medium-high heat (400°F to 450°F/205°C to 230°C) and lightly oil the grates.

Pour the remaining oil into a medium bowl and add ½ teaspoon salt. Add the grapes and halved shallots and toss to coat. Thread the grapes onto the skewers and set aside. Add a generous pinch of pepper to the shallots and toss to coat. Set aside.

Place the chicken and the shallots cut-side down on the grill and cook undisturbed for 3 to 5 minutes, until they easily release from the grates.

Flip the chicken and shallots and cook for an additional 3 to 5 minutes, until cooked through. Add the grapes to the grill and cook, turning occasionally, until they have char marks and are slightly softened, 1 to 2 minutes.

Remove the chicken, shallots, and grapes from the grill. Slice the chicken and place it on a serving platter. Carefully remove the grapes from the skewers using tongs and arrange them over the chicken. Tuck in the grilled shallots and top with the chives. Serve immediately.

SPECIAL EQUIPMENT:
6 to 8 metal or wooden skewers

½ cup (120 ml) olive oil, divided

Zest of 1 lemon

3 cloves garlic, chopped

2 teaspoons Dijon mustard

1 teaspoon dried oregano

Kosher salt and freshly ground black pepper

4 (6- to 8-ounce/170 to 225 g) boneless, skinless chicken breasts, lightly pounded to ½-inch (1.25 cm) thickness

1 heaping cup (165 g) green seedless grapes

1 heaping cup (165 g) red seedless grapes

4 shallots, peeled with root end intact, then sliced in half lengthwise

2 tablespoons sliced fresh chives

PRO TIP: If using wooden skewers, be sure to soak them in water for at least 30 minutes before use.

Spicy Soy
CHICKEN KEBABS

PREP TIME: 10 minutes   **MARINATING TIME:** 30 minutes to 6 hours   **COOK TIME:** 15 minutes   **YIELD:** Serves 6

I've already professed my love for easy, quick-cooking, crowd-pleasing kebabs, so it only makes sense to give you yet another recipe. This time we're shellacking cubes of juicy thigh meat (the best bits for kebabs, by the way) with a spicy soy glaze. But if you're not big on heat, just reduce or omit the sambal.

SPECIAL EQUIPMENT:

6 to 8 metal or wooden skewers

½ cup (120 ml) reduced-sodium
   soy sauce

2 teaspoons toasted sesame oil

1 tablespoon neutral oil,
   such as avocado or grapeseed

2 teaspoons sambal oelek

½ teaspoon Chinese five-spice
   powder

2 pounds (910 g) boneless, skinless
   chicken thighs, cut into 1-inch
   (2.5 cm) cubes

2 bunches green onions, light green
   parts cut into 1-inch (2.5 cm)
   pieces, dark green parts thinly
   sliced and reserved for garnish

Toasted sesame seeds, for garnish

Put the soy sauce, oils, sambal, and five-spice powder in a large bowl and whisk to combine. Add the chicken and toss to coat with the marinade. Cover the bowl and let sit in the refrigerator for 30 minutes to 6 hours.

Once the chicken has marinated, assemble the skewers. Thread pieces of chicken onto the skewers, alternating with a few pieces of green onion.

Preheat a gas or charcoal grill to medium heat (350°F to 400°F/175°C to 204°C) and lightly oil the grates.

Place the kebabs on the grill and cook for 10 to 15 minutes, turning every few minutes to cook evenly, until the internal temperature of the chicken reaches 165°F (74°C).

Transfer the chicken to a platter and garnish with the dark green parts of the green onions and toasted sesame seeds.

PRO TIP: If using wooden skewers, be sure to soak them in water for at least 30 minutes before use.

Chipotle Lime
CHICKEN THIGHS

PREP TIME: 10 minutes **MARINATING TIME:** 30 minutes to 4 hours **COOK TIME:** 10 minutes **YIELD:** Serves 4

Growing up in Arizona and living in California means that Mexican-inspired flavors run deep with me. I've always loved the way the smoky spice of chiles deepens the flavor of whatever it is you're cooking them with, and how a bright hit of lime wakes up a dish and makes everything taste more like itself—only better. So I'm teaming up these magic ingredients for this otherwise super-simple chicken thigh recipe, which would be perfect with a salad or, if you're an overachiever like me, in some quesadillas or tacos.

Preheat one half of the grill to medium-high heat (400°F to 450°F/205°C to 230°C) and lightly oil the grates. If using charcoal, set up the briquettes underneath half of the grill grate.

Put the chipotles, adobo sauce, lime juice, oil, honey, cumin, coriander, smoked paprika, salt, and pepper in a large bowl and whisk to combine. Add the chicken thighs and toss to coat in the marinade. Cover the bowl and let marinate in the refrigerator for 30 minutes and up to 4 hours.

Place the chicken on the grill, skin-side down, and cook for 2 to 3 minutes, until nice grill marks form and the chicken skin is nicely browned. Flip the chicken and cook for an additional 3 minutes. Transfer the chicken to the unlit side of the grill, cover, and cook until the internal temperature reaches 165°F (74°C).

Transfer the chicken to a platter, garnish with cilantro leaves, and serve with lime wedges.

3 chipotle chiles in adobo, chopped

2 tablespoons adobo sauce (from the can of chipotles)

¼ cup (60 ml) fresh lime juice

2 tablespoons olive oil

2 tablespoons honey

2 teaspoons ground cumin

1 teaspoon ground coriander

1 teaspoon smoked paprika

1½ teaspoons kosher salt

½ teaspoon freshly ground black pepper

2 pounds (910 g) bone-in, skin-on chicken thighs (6 to 8 thighs)

Fresh cilantro leaves, for garnish

Lime wedges, for serving

CHICKEN SATAY with Peanut Sauce and Smashed Cucumber Salad

PREP TIME: 25 minutes   **MARINATING TIME:** 30 minutes   **COOK TIME:** 10 minutes   **YIELD:** Serves 4 to 6

I love traveling through food because it means either bringing home a piece of a place I've visited and loved or getting to feel like I'm somewhere I haven't gotten to go yet. For these tenders, which get marinated in a Southeast Asian–inspired blend of soy sauce, fish sauce, ginger, and lime juice and served alongside a sweet-salty peanut dipping sauce and refreshing vinegar-spiked smashed cucumbers, we're taking off for Indonesia.

SPECIAL EQUIPMENT:

6 to 8 metal or wooden skewers

FOR THE CHICKEN:

⅓ cup (70 ml) reduced-sodium
   soy sauce

2 tablespoons neutral oil,
   such as avocado or grapeseed

2 teaspoons fish sauce

Zest and juice of 1 lime

2 teaspoons light brown sugar

2 teaspoons ground ginger

1 teaspoon onion powder

1 teaspoon garlic powder

1 teaspoon red pepper flakes

1 teaspoon ground turmeric

1½ pounds (680 g) chicken tenders

FOR THE PEANUT SAUCE:

½ cup (125 g) creamy peanut butter

1 tablespoon fresh lime juice

2 tablespoons reduced-sodium
   soy sauce

1 tablespoon rice vinegar

1 teaspoon grated fresh ginger

2 teaspoons honey

FOR THE CUCUMBER SALAD:

2 tablespoons reduced-sodium
   soy sauce

1 tablespoon rice vinegar

1 teaspoon toasted sesame oil

2 cloves garlic, grated

1 teaspoon granulated sugar

1 teaspoon dashi powder

1 pound (455 g) Persian cucumbers

½ cup (52 g) thinly sliced red onion

2 tablespoons toasted sesame seeds

TO PREPARE THE CHICKEN: Put the soy sauce, oil, fish sauce, lime zest, lime juice, brown sugar, ground ginger, onion powder, garlic powder, red pepper flakes, and turmeric in a large bowl and whisk to combine. Add the chicken tenders and toss to coat in the marinade. Cover the bowl and let marinate for 30 minutes at room temperature.

Preheat a gas or charcoal grill to medium heat (350°F to 450°F/175°C to 230°C) and lightly oil the grates.

TO MAKE THE PEANUT SAUCE: Put all of the ingredients in a small bowl and whisk to combine. If the sauce is too thick, add water, 1 tablespoon at a time, until the sauce is your desired consistency. Refrigerate until ready to serve.

TO MAKE THE CUCUMBER SALAD: Put the soy sauce, vinegar, sesame oil, garlic, sugar, and dashi powder in a large bowl and whisk to combine. Slice off the ends of the cucumbers and cut in half lengthwise. With a spoon or flat meat mallet, gently smash the cucumbers until they split and the entire length of the cucumbers are smashed, then break them into 1-inch (2.5 cm) pieces. Add the cucumber and onion to the dressing and mix to combine. Garnish with the sesame seeds and set aside until ready to serve.

After the 30 minutes of marinating, skewer the chicken. Thread the chicken tenders onto the skewers, letting any excess marinade drip back into the bowl.

Place the skewers onto the grill and cook for 3 to 4 minutes per side, until cooked through and the internal temperature is 165°F (74°C).

Transfer the satay to a platter and serve with the peanut sauce and smashed cucumber salad.

PRO TIP: If using wooden skewers, be sure to soak them in water for at least 30 minutes before use.

Grilled Curry
DRUMSTICKS with Raita

PREP TIME: 20 minutes **MARINATING TIME:** 2 to 8 hours **COOK TIME:** 20 minutes **YIELD:** Serves 4

Raita is a traditional Indian yogurt-based condiment that's similar to tzatziki. Aside from their fresh, tangy flavors, another thing these two sauces have in common is that they're delicious on just about anything, and they stay nice and cool when a situation gets a little bit spicy. While these drumsticks don't necessarily bring the heat, they are spiced with curry powder, cumin, and turmeric. I especially love cooking them over charcoal because of how it makes the skin extra crispy, but no matter what, you need to serve them with a dollop of raita for a meal that hits every angle of your taste buds.

TO MARINATE THE CHICKEN: Put the yogurt, oil, curry powder, turmeric, chipotle chile powder, cumin, salt, and pepper in a large bowl and whisk until combined. Add the drumsticks and thoroughly mix to coat the chicken in the yogurt mixture. Cover the bowl and let marinate in the refrigerator for at least 2 hours or up to 8 hours.

TO MAKE THE RAITA: Put all of the ingredients in a bowl and mix to combine. Refrigerate until ready to serve.

Remove the chicken from the marinade and wipe off most of the excess yogurt mixture.

Set up a gas or charcoal grill for indirect cooking by preheating one half of the grill to medium-high heat (400°F to 450°F/205°C to 230°C) and lightly oil the grates. If using charcoal, set up the briquettes underneath half of the grill grate.

Place the drumsticks on the grill and cook for 5 to 7 minutes, until nice grill marks form and the chicken skin is nicely browned. Flip the chicken and cook for an additional 5 minutes. Transfer the chicken to the unlit side of the grill, cover, and cook until the internal temperature reaches 165°F (74°C).

Transfer the chicken to a serving platter, top with mint leaves, and serve with lime wedges and raita.

FOR THE CHICKEN:

1 cup (240 ml) plain yogurt
¼ cup (60 ml) olive oil
1 tablespoon curry powder
2 teaspoons ground turmeric
1 teaspoon chipotle chile powder
1 teaspoon ground cumin
2 teaspoons kosher salt
1 teaspoon freshly ground
  black pepper
8 chicken drumsticks
  (about 2 pounds/910 g)

FOR THE RAITA:

1 cup (240 ml) plain yogurt
1 tablespoon fresh lemon juice
1 Persian cucumber, skin on,
  finely chopped
1 Roma tomato, seeds removed
  and chopped
⅓ cup (17 g) finely chopped white
  onion (from ½ small onion)
2 tablespoons finely chopped
  fresh cilantro
Kosher salt and freshly ground black
  pepper to taste

Fresh mint leaves, for garnish
Lime wedges, for serving

Grilled Shawarma-Style
CHICKEN with Fattoush Salad

PREP TIME: 30 minutes   **MARINATING TIME:** 30 minutes to 8 hours   **COOK TIME:** 15 minutes   **YIELD:** Serves 6 to 8

When I was thirteen, my parents took me to Turkey. And as much as it pains me to admit it, I was still in my picky eating phase. (Does it count as a phase if it lasts for twenty years?) Needless to say, my experience of all the incredible Middle Eastern/Mediterranean foods there was pretty much limited. I obviously need a do-over, but until then, I comfort myself with this recipe that's inspired by foods from the region.

FOR THE CHICKEN:

1 teaspoon ground cumin

1 teaspoon ground coriander

1 teaspoon smoked paprika

1 teaspoon chipotle chile powder

½ teaspoon red pepper flakes

¼ teaspoon ground ginger

¼ teaspoon ground cinnamon

⅓ cup (70 ml) olive oil

Kosher salt

2 pounds (910 g) boneless, skinless chicken thighs

FOR THE GRILLED PITA AND FATTOUSH SALAD:

2 teaspoons smoked paprika

½ teaspoon ground cumin

Kosher salt

¼ cup (60 ml) plus 3 tablespoons olive oil

2 pita breads

¼ cup (60 ml) red wine vinegar

2 teaspoons Dijon mustard

1 teaspoon dried oregano

Freshly ground black pepper

3 vine tomatoes, chopped

3 Persian cucumbers, chopped

5 to 7 radishes, cut into chunky matchsticks

½ small red onion, thinly sliced

¼ cup (15 g) chopped fresh dill

¼ cup (15 g) chopped fresh parsley

3 lemons, cut in half

TO MARINATE THE CHICKEN: Put the cumin, coriander, smoked paprika, chipotle chile powder, red pepper flakes, ground ginger, cinnamon, oil, and 2 teaspoons salt in a large bowl and whisk to combine. Add the chicken thighs to the spice mixture and toss to evenly coat the chicken in the marinade. Cover and let marinate for 30 minutes at room temperature or up to 8 hours in the refrigerator.

Preheat a gas or charcoal grill to medium-high heat (400°F to 450°F/205°C to 230°C) and lightly oil the grates.

TO MAKE THE GRILLED PITA AND FATTOUSH SALAD: Put the smoked paprika, cumin, ½ teaspoon salt, and 3 tablespoons of the oil in a small bowl and whisk to combine. Brush the pita with the spiced oil. Place the whole pita onto the grill and toast on both sides until lightly browned. Remove from the grill and tear into pieces.

Put the remaining ¼ cup (60 ml) oil, the vinegar, mustard, oregano, and a generous pinch of salt and pepper in a salad bowl and whisk to combine. Add the tomatoes, cucumbers, radishes, onion, and fresh herbs to the dressing and toss to combine.

Place the chicken on the grill in an even layer and cook for 5 minutes, or until the chicken has nice grill marks and easily releases from the grill. Flip the chicken and cook for another 5 to 7 minutes, until the internal temperature reaches 165°F (74°C). Let the chicken rest for 5 to 10 minutes.

Lightly oil the halved lemons and grill, cut-side down, until charred, 3 to 5 minutes. Remove the lemons to a serving platter. Slice the chicken and add it to the serving platter. Toss the salad to coat in the dressing, top with the crispy pita and a few squeezes of the grilled lemons, and serve.

PRO TIP: If using wooden skewers, be sure to soak them in water for at least 30 minutes before use.

Dinner party: SMOKE SHOW

There's a cookout and then there's a COOKOUT, when you go even bigger and bolder in the flavor department. From the cheddar smoked pigs in a blanket to carrots with romesco sauce to strawberry rhubarb biscuit cobbler, this is the perfect menu for proving that everything—and I mean everything—is better with smoke. Serve with a round (or three) of spicy smoky margaritas.

Cheddar Smoked
PIGS IN A BLANKET

PREP TIME: 25 minutes   **COOK TIME:** 40 minutes   **YIELD:** Serves 4 to 6

Preheat a pellet grill or smoker to 350°F (175°C). Spray a sheet pan that will fit in the grill with nonstick cooking spray and set aside.

Put the poppy seeds and salt in a small bowl and mix to combine. In a separate small bowl, whisk the egg with a splash of water to combine. Set both bowls aside.

Prep the cheese by cutting each slice into 8 equal long strips. Open the can of crescent dough and separate into triangles. Cut each triangle lengthwise into 3 smaller triangles.

To assemble the pigs in a blanket, use a pastry brush to add a thin layer of honey mustard to each of the triangles. Place a strip of cheese on top of the mustard. Place a cocktail sausage on the wide end of the dough and roll up, pinching to seal the end. Place on the prepared sheet pan. Repeat with the remaining ingredients.

Brush the tops of the pigs in a blanket with the egg wash and sprinkle with the poppy seed and salt mixture.

Transfer the pan to the pellet grill and close the lid. Cook for 25 to 30 minutes, until puffed and golden brown. Let cool for 10 minutes. Serve with ketchup.

Nonstick cooking spray

1 tablespoon poppy seeds

2 teaspoons kosher salt

1 large egg

3 (4-inch/10 cm square) deli slices sharp Cheddar cheese

1 (8-ounce/226 g) can crescent roll dough

3 tablespoons honey mustard

1 (14-ounce/396 g) package cocktail sausages, thoroughly dried

Ketchup, for serving

Smoked Spatchcock
CHICKEN

PREP TIME: 20 minutes   **COOK TIME:** 1 hour   **YIELD:** Serves 4 to 6

---

1 tablespoon light brown sugar

1 tablespoon onion powder

1 tablespoon garlic powder

2 teaspoons smoked paprika

1 teaspoon chipotle chile powder

1 tablespoon smoked salt
(such as Maldon)

1 teaspoon freshly ground
black pepper

1 (5-pound/2.25 kg) whole chicken

2 tablespoons olive oil

2 lemons, cut into wedges

Preheat a pellet smoker to 400°F (204°C), load the hopper with wood pellets, and let it heat up with the lid closed for at least 15 minutes.

Put the brown sugar, onion powder, garlic powder, smoked paprika, chipotle chile powder, smoked salt, and pepper in a small bowl and mix well to combine. Set aside.

Remove any giblets from inside the chicken and discard them. Place the chicken, breast-side down, on a clean work surface. Use kitchen shears to cut along either side of the backbone to remove it. Turn the chicken over so it is now breast-side up. Use your hands to firmly press down on the breastbone to break it. This will enable the chicken to lie flat. Pat both sides of the chicken dry with a paper towel.

Using clean hands or a silicone brush, coat the entire chicken with the oil. Season the chicken on both sides with the seasoning blend.

Place the chicken directly on the grill grates, breast-side up. Cook for 50 to 60 minutes, until the chicken reaches 160°F (71°C). Remove the chicken from the smoker and let it rest for 10 minutes. The internal temperature will come up to 165°F (74°C) as it rests.

Cut the chicken into pieces and place on a serving platter. Serve with lemon wedges.

Smoked CARROTS

with Romesco Sauce

PREP TIME: 20 minutes   **COOK TIME:** 35 minutes   **YIELD:** Serves 4 to 6

Preheat a pellet smoker to 400°F (205°C), load the hopper with wood pellets, and let it heat up with the lid closed for at least 15 minutes.

Put 2 tablespoons oil, ½ teaspoon of the smoked paprika, and a generous pinch of salt and pepper in a large bowl and whisk to combine. Add the carrots to the bowl and toss to coat them in the seasoning.

Transfer the carrots to the smoker and cook, turning every 10 minutes, until they are tender, 25 to 35 minutes.

Meanwhile, make the romesco sauce: Combine the peppers, toasted almonds, vinegar, remaining ½ teaspoon smoked paprika, the red pepper flakes, basil, garlic, and ½ teaspoon salt in a food processor and pulse until mostly smooth. With the machine running, stream in ⅓ cup (70 ml) oil through the hole in the lid and blend until smooth. Taste and season with salt and pepper as needed.

Remove the carrots to a cutting board and cut into large chunks, if desired; otherwise, serve whole. Transfer to a serving platter and top with some of the romesco sauce. Garnish with chives and parsley. Serve extra sauce on the side.

Olive oil

1 teaspoon smoked paprika, divided

Kosher salt and freshly ground black pepper

2 pounds (910 g) multicolor carrots, trimmed

4 whole roasted bell peppers (see page 146), thoroughly dried

¾ cup (69 g) sliced almonds, toasted

3 tablespoons red wine vinegar

½ teaspoon red pepper flakes

¼ cup (20 g) fresh basil leaves

2 cloves garlic, roughly chopped

Chopped fresh chives, for garnish

Chopped fresh parsley, for garnish

COUSCOUS SALAD

with Sun-Dried Tomato Vinaigrette

PREP TIME: 15 minutes   **COOK TIME:** 10 minutes   **YIELD:** Serves 4 to 6

Kosher salt

1½ cups (270 g) Israeli couscous

⅓ cup (40 g) sun-dried tomatoes in olive oil, drained

¼ cup (60 ml) red wine vinegar

2 teaspoons Dijon mustard

2 teaspoons dried oregano

2 cloves garlic, peeled

⅓ cup (70 ml) olive oil

Freshly ground black pepper

1 (15-ounce/425 g) can chickpeas, rinsed and drained

½ cup (75 g) crumbled feta cheese

⅓ cup (35 g) chopped fresh parsley

2 tablespoons fresh lemon juice

Bring a pot of salted water to a boil. Add the couscous and cook until tender, 8 to 10 minutes. Drain and transfer to a large bowl.

To make the dressing, combine the sun-dried tomatoes, vinegar, mustard, oregano, garlic, oil, ½ teaspoon salt, and ¼ teaspoon pepper in a high-powered blender and blend until completely smooth.

Add the dressing, chickpeas, cheese, parsley, and lemon juice to the bowl with the cooked couscous. Mix well to combine and season with salt and pepper. Serve immediately or cover and store in the fridge until ready to serve.

Spicy Smoky MARGARITA

PREP TIME: 10 minutes **YIELD:** Makes 1 drink

Combine the smoky salt and chile powder in a small shallow dish and stir to evenly combine. Make a vertical slice in the lime wedge pulp so that it sits on the edge of the glass. Slide the lime around the rim of the glass to coat it in lime juice. Dip the rim of the glass in the salt mixture and tap off any excess. Reserve the lime wedge for garnish. Set the glass aside in the freezer while you make the margarita.

To make the margarita, add ice to a shaker. Top the ice with the tequila, triple sec, lime juice, agave, and jalapeño slices. Place the lid on the shaker and shake vigorously until the shaker is cold and frosty on the outside, 20 to 30 seconds.

Remove the rimmed glass from the freezer and fill with ice. Strain the margarita over the ice and garnish with the lime wedge. Serve immediately.

2 teaspoons smoked salt

½ teaspoon single-origin chile powder

Lime wedge

2 ounces (60 ml) silver tequila

1 ounce (30 ml) triple sec

1½ ounces (45 ml) fresh lime juice

½ ounce (15 ml) agave nectar

3 slices jalapeño

Smoked Strawberry Rhubarb
BISCUIT COBBLER

PREP TIME: 20 minutes   **COOK TIME:** 50 minutes   **YIELD:** Serves 6

FOR THE COBBLER BASE:

7 cups (1.2 kg) fresh strawberries, hulled and cut in half

4 cups (400 g) chopped fresh rhubarb (1-inch/2.5 cm pieces)

1 cup (200 g) granulated sugar

¼ cup (45 g) quick-cooking tapioca

1 vanilla bean pod, seeds scraped

1 tablespoon orange zest

2 tablespoons fresh orange juice

¼ teaspoon kosher salt

FOR THE BISCUIT TOPPING:

1⅔ cups (165 g) all-purpose flour, plus more for kneading

½ cup (100 g) granulated sugar

½ cup (75 g) fine-ground cornmeal

2½ teaspoons baking powder

¼ teaspoon kosher salt

7 tablespoons cold unsalted butter, cut into small pieces

⅔ cup (170 ml) buttermilk, plus more to brush on the biscuits

¼ cup (63 g) raw or coarse sugar

Whipped cream or vanilla ice cream, for serving

Preheat a pellet smoker (or your oven) to 350° (175°C), load the hopper with wood pellets, and let it heat up with the lid closed for at least 15 minutes. Grease a 10- to 12-inch (25 to 30 cm) cast-iron skillet or enamel cast-iron pan and set aside.

TO MAKE THE COBBLER BASE: Place the strawberries, rhubarb, sugar, tapioca, vanilla and scraped pods, orange zest, orange juice, and salt in a large bowl and stir to combine. Place directly into the prepared pan.

TO MAKE THE BISCUIT TOPPING: Whisk together the flour, granulated sugar, cornmeal, baking powder, and salt in a medium bowl. Cut in the butter with your fingers or a pastry blender until the mixture looks like coarse meal with pea-size bits of butter. Add the buttermilk and stir with a fork until a shaggy dough forms. Turn the dough out onto a lightly floured surface and knead a few times to bring it together. Quickly fold the dough over itself a few times to help create layers. Pat into an even 8-inch (20 cm) square. Cut the biscuits into 2-inch (5 cm) squares with a knife.

Arrange the biscuits on top of the filling. Brush with buttermilk and sprinkle with coarse sugar. Place the cobbler onto the pellet smoker and bake until the biscuits are golden and the filling is bubbling, about 50 minutes.

Remove from the pellet smoker, pull out the vanilla bean pods, and let rest for 15 to 20 minutes. Serve with whipped cream or vanilla ice cream.

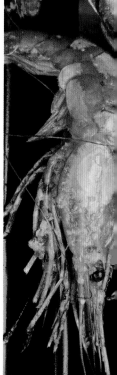

SEAFOOD

From the time I was cooking as a private chef and just starting to share recipes online, the most common thing I heard from people who enjoyed one of my seafood-centered meals was "I wish I could cook my own great fish and seafood dishes at home." And because doing just that is way too easy for there to be this much self-doubt, I've made it my mission to clear up all the mysteries. But this chapter takes the simplicity to a whole new level because there's nothing fish and shellfish love more than a quick hit of high heat. Plus, everything from salmon to shrimp to clams to oysters—yes, oysters!—soaks up all that smoke plus any marinade you throw their way. The effect is the ultimate in sophistication with truly minimal fuss. In other words: You got this!

Charred
FISH TACOS with Chipotle Crema

PREP TIME: 20 minutes   **MARINATING TIME:** 2 hours   **COOK TIME:** 12 minutes   **YIELD:** Serves 4

If I had to pick a last meal, fish tacos would be involved. And while I love all fish tacos—battered, fried, breaded, grilled, seared, etc.—these grilled tacos with a chipotle crema are truly next level. The slaw is also perfection, and you'll want to make a triple batch so you can eat it as a salad too.

FOR THE SLAW:

⅓ head red cabbage, shredded (about 1½ cups/100 g)

½ medium yellow onion, thinly sliced

½ cup (120 ml) apple cider vinegar or red wine vinegar

¼ cup (60 ml) water

½ teaspoon kosher salt

1 teaspoon dried oregano

1 teaspoon red pepper flakes

FOR THE CHIPOTLE CREMA:

1 cup (240 ml) sour cream or Mexican crema

Zest and juice of ½ medium lime

3 tablespoons adobo sauce (from canned chipotles in adobo)

½ teaspoon kosher salt, or to taste

FOR THE FISH:

1¼ pounds (570 g) sea bass

Olive oil, for drizzling

Kosher salt and freshly cracked black pepper

½ teaspoon cayenne pepper

½ teaspoon garlic powder

½ teaspoon ground cumin

1 lime

1 orange

FOR SERVING:

8 to 10 corn or flour tortillas, warmed or charred

Guacamole (page 228)

TO MAKE THE SLAW: Combine the cabbage and onion in a large bowl. Whisk together the vinegar, water, salt, oregano, and red pepper flakes in a small bowl. Pour over the cabbage mixture and toss to fully coat. Cover and refrigerate for at least 2 hours before serving. Slaw can be prepped ahead up to 6 hours max before it starts to get a bit too soft.

TO MAKE THE CHIPOTLE CREMA: Combine all the ingredients for the crema and taste. Adjust seasoning as needed and set aside.

TO GRILL THE FISH: Preheat a gas or charcoal grill to medium-high heat (400°F to 450°F/205°C to 230°C) and lightly oil the grates.

Drizzle the sea bass with a touch of oil and season with salt, pepper, the cayenne, garlic powder, and cumin. Grill the fish for 5 to 6 minutes on each side, until the fish is fully cooked and flakes easily and there is a golden brown crust.

Remove the fish from the grill and squeeze the juice from the lime and orange over the fish. Transfer to a bowl and use 2 forks to gently flake the fish into large chunks. Adjust the salt and pepper as needed.

To assemble, place a few large pieces of the flaked fish into a warmed tortilla. Top with a spoonful of guacamole, some chipotle crema, and 2 tablespoons of the slaw. Serve immediately.

Grilled
SHRIMP
and Charred Chopped Salad

PREP TIME: 15 minutes **MARINATING TIME:** 1 to 6 hours **COOK TIME:** 6 minutes **YIELD:** Serves 4 to 6

If you're not charring your lettuce, are you even living your best life? Giving your lettuce a quick sear on the grill offers a salad yet another layer of flavor, which is a no-brainer if you already have the grill going to cook up some shrimp. Toss it all together with sweet corn, avocado, stone fruit, and my basil vinaigrette, and you have the ultimate summer salad.

TO MARINATE THE SHRIMP: Season the shrimp with salt and pepper. Whisk together the oil, vinegar, garlic, lemon zest, lemon juice, and soy sauce in a medium bowl. Add the shrimp, toss to coat, cover, and marinate in the refrigerator for at least 1 hour or up to 6 hours.

Preheat a gas or charcoal grill to medium-high heat (400°F to 450°F/205°C to 230°C) and lightly oil the grates.

TO MAKE THE BASIL VINAIGRETTE: Combine all the ingredients in a high-powered blender and blend for 1 minute, or until very smooth. Taste and adjust the salt and black pepper as needed. If making in advance, cover and refrigerate the vinaigrette for up to 5 days.

TO GRILL THE SHRIMP: Thread the shrimp on the skewers. Place on the grill and grill on each side for about 2 minutes, until cooked through. Discard the marinade.

TO MAKE THE SALAD: Once the shrimp is cooked, drizzle the lettuce and corn with oil. Grill the lettuce and corn for 1 to 2 minutes, until there are char marks on the lettuce but it still holds its shape and the corn is charred. Remove from the grill. Chop the lettuce and remove the kernels from the corn.

Combine the shrimp, lettuce, corn, avocado, and stone fruit in a serving bowl. Drizzle with a few tablespoons of the basil vinaigrette and serve.

SPECIAL EQUIPMENT:

6 metal or wooden skewers

FOR THE SHRIMP:

1 pound (455 g) large shrimp, peeled and deveined

Kosher salt and freshly ground black pepper

½ cup (120 ml) olive oil

¼ cup (60 ml) red wine vinegar

6 cloves garlic, minced

1 teaspoon lemon zest

1 tablespoon fresh lemon juice

2 tablespoons soy sauce

FOR THE BASIL VINAIGRETTE:

1 shallot, roughly chopped

2 cups (about 4 ounces/115 g) tightly packed fresh basil leaves

1 clove garlic, peeled

½ teaspoon red pepper flakes

½ cup (120 ml) olive oil

2 tablespoons red wine vinegar

1 teaspoon kosher salt

½ teaspoon freshly ground black pepper

FOR THE SALAD:

4 to 5 small heads romaine lettuce

2 ears corn, shucked

Olive oil, for drizzling

1 to 2 avocados, diced

2 to 3 stone fruits, cut into wedges

PRO TIP: If using wooden skewers, be sure to soak them in water for at least 30 minutes before use.

Cedar plank
SALMON with Tartar Sauce

PREP TIME: 25 minutes   **COOK TIME:** 15 minutes   **YIELD:** Serves 4

Cedar planks are one of my secrets to nailing perfectly cooked fish every time I grill. Because you're not laying the fish directly on the grates, there's zero risk of it sticking, and because you're using indirect heat, you have a little more wiggle room with cook times. Plus, serving the salmon right off the plank with a homemade tartar sauce makes such an impressive presentation. To infuse your fish with a little extra zip, soak your plank in white wine before putting it on the grill.

SPECIAL EQUIPMENT:
1 or 2 cedar planks (depending on the size of your fillets)

FOR THE TARTAR SAUCE:
1 cup (240 ml) mayonnaise

1 tablespoon chopped dill pickles or relish

1 tablespoon capers, chopped

1 tablespoon chopped fresh dill

1 teaspoon lemon zest

1 tablespoon fresh lemon juice

Kosher salt and freshly ground black pepper, to taste

FOR THE COMPOUND BUTTER:
⅓ cup (75 g) unsalted butter

4 green onions, white and light green parts only, thinly sliced

2 cloves garlic, grated

Zest and juice of 1 lemon

¼ teaspoon kosher salt

¼ teaspoon freshly ground black pepper

FOR THE SALMON:
4 (6- to 8-ounce/170 to 225 g) skin-on salmon fillets

Arugula, for serving (optional)

Kosher salt and freshly ground black pepper

Lemon wedges, for serving

TO MAKE THE TARTAR SAUCE: Place all the ingredients in a small bowl and whisk to combine. Cover and refrigerate until ready to serve.

TO MAKE THE COMPOUND BUTTER: Melt the butter in a small saucepan over medium heat. Turn the heat down to low and add the green onions, garlic, lemon zest, lemon juice, salt, and pepper. Stir to combine. Cook until the garlic is fragrant, about 1 minute. Remove from the heat and set aside to cool to room temperature.

TO GRILL THE SALMON: Soak the cedar planks in water or white wine for 30 minutes before use.

Preheat a gas or charcoal grill to medium heat (350°F to 400°F/175°C to 204°C). Arrange some arugula on a platter, if using, and set aside.

Once the grill is preheated, remove the cedar planks from the water and pat dry with paper towels. Place the fish on the planks, skin-side down. Season the fish with salt and pepper and transfer to the grill. Drizzle a tablespoon or so of the compound butter on each piece of fish. Close the grill and cook for 10 to 15 minutes, until the fish is opaque and easily flakes with a fork.

Remove the planks from the grill and serve directly on the planks or on the bed of arugula. Drizzle the remaining butter over the fish. Serve with lemon wedges and tartar sauce.

Sausage and
SHRIMP PAELLA

PREP TIME: 20 minutes   **COOK TIME:** 30 minutes   **YIELD:** Serves 6 to 8

This is one of my favorite recipes from my private chef days. I still love nothing more than throwing a paella party where everyone digs in to a big, gorgeous platter full of pepper- and tomato-flecked rice and loads of smoky shrimp and sausage. Add a few bottles of your favorite Spanish Rioja and you're in business.

Preheat a gas or charcoal grill to medium heat (350°F to 400°F/175°C to 204°C) and lightly oil the grates.

Combine the shrimp, lemon zest, and 1 tablespoon of the oil in a large bowl. Season with salt and pepper and toss to combine. Transfer the shrimp to the grill in an even layer and reserve the marinade (it will be only a small spoonful). Cook for 2 to 3 minutes, until nice char marks form. Flip and continue to cook for another minute or two, until the shrimp are pink and cooked through. Remove to a plate and set aside.

Heat a 12-inch (30 cm) paella pan on the grill. Add 2 tablespoons of the remaining oil and the sausage. Cook for 6 to 8 minutes, until the sausage is browned on both sides. Use a slotted spoon to remove the sausage to the plate with the shrimp and set aside.

Add the onion and bell peppers to the pan and cook, stirring often for 5 minutes, or until the vegetables are softened. Add the garlic, tomatoes, reserved shrimp marinade, and parsley and cook just until the garlic is fragrant, about 1 minute.

Add the remaining 1 tablespoon oil to the pan along with the rice. Stir to coat the rice in the oil and vegetables and cook for 2 to 3 minutes, until the rice is slightly toasted. Add 4 cups (960 ml) of the chicken stock, 1 cup (240 ml) at a time, and cook, stirring frequently, until the rice is al dente, 15 to 20 minutes. If the rice is a bit too al dente for your preference, add another 1 to 2 cups (240 to 480 ml) stock until you've reached your desired consistency.

Arrange the shrimp and sausage in the rice. Turn the grill off and close the lid just to warm everything through. Remove the paella pan from the grill. Garnish with parsley and serve with lemon wedges.

1 pound (455 g) large shrimp, peeled and deveined, tails intact

1 teaspoon lemon zest

4 tablespoons neutral oil, such as avocado or grapeseed, divided

Kosher salt and freshly ground black pepper

1 pound (455 g) smoked sausage, such as kielbasa or andouille, cut into rounds

1 medium yellow onion, diced

1 red bell pepper, diced

1 yellow bell pepper, diced

5 cloves garlic, chopped

2 Roma tomatoes, chopped

¼ cup (15 g) chopped fresh parsley, plus more for garnish

2 cups (195 g) short-grain white rice

4 to 6 cups (960 ml to 1.4 L) chicken stock

Lemon wedges, for serving

Grilled Ginger
GARLIC SHRIMP
with Coconut Green Goddess Dressing

PREP TIME: 20 minutes   **MARINATING TIME:** 10 minutes   **COOK TIME:** 6 minutes   **YIELD:** Serves 4 to 6

Sometimes my recipes start with the protein as inspiration, and sometimes they start with a sauce that I need to pair with something else because drinking it straight up isn't a great dinner option. In this case, my obsession began with coconut green goddess dressing, which blends the classic fresh herb flavors with Southeast Asian pops of cilantro, fish sauce, and lime. It would be delicious on pretty much anything—seafood, chicken, naan—but it is particularly divine on these jumbo shrimp.

SPECIAL EQUIPMENT:

6 metal or wooden skewers

FOR THE QUICK PICKLED SPICY CARROTS:

½ cup (120 ml) distilled white vinegar

½ cup (120 ml) rice vinegar

1 cup (240 ml) water

¼ cup (50 g) granulated sugar

1 teaspoon kosher salt

1½ cups (180 g) julienned carrots (1 to 2 large carrots)

1 serrano chile, very thinly sliced

FOR THE COCONUT GREEN GODDESS DRESSING:

½ bunch cilantro

5 large fresh basil leaves

10 large fresh mint leaves, plus more for garnish

1 small shallot, roughly chopped

½ small serrano chile, seeds removed, roughly chopped

1 (1-inch/2.5 cm) piece fresh ginger, grated

½ cup (120 ml) full-fat coconut milk

1 tablespoon honey

2 tablespoons rice vinegar

Juice of 1 lime, or to taste

1 teaspoon fish sauce

(ingredients continue)

TO MAKE THE QUICK PICKLED SPICY CARROTS: Combine the white vinegar, rice vinegar, water, sugar, and salt in a medium pot and bring to a boil over high heat, stirring to dissolve the sugar and salt. This is your brine.

While the brine is heating, place the carrots and chiles in a 1-pint (480 ml) Mason jar or small heatproof bowl.

When the brine comes to a boil, carefully pour it over the carrots and chiles, leaving about 1 inch (2.5 cm) of space at the top of the jar. You'll have a little brine left over. Let the jar cool to room temperature, then secure the lid and transfer to the fridge. The quick pickled carrots can be eaten immediately, but the flavor improves with a few hours in the fridge. Use within 2 weeks.

TO MAKE THE COCONUT GREEN GODDESS DRESSING: Combine all the ingredients in a blender and blend until smooth. Taste and adjust with more salt, pepper, and/or lime juice.

TO MARINATE THE SHRIMP: Whisk together the oil, ginger, chile, lime zest, lime juice, and garlic in a large bowl. Season with salt and pepper. Gently pry the shrimp shells apart to open them up. Place in the marinade and rub the marinade all over the shrimp. Season with more salt and pepper. Let sit on the counter for 10 minutes.

(recipe continues)

1 tablespoon olive oil

Kosher salt and freshly ground
  black pepper

FOR THE SHRIMP:

¼ cup (60 ml) olive oil

2 teaspoons finely grated fresh ginger

½ serrano chile, finely minced
  (seeds removed if you want it
  less spicy)

1 tablespoon lime zest

2 tablespoons fresh lime juice

4 cloves garlic, finely grated

Kosher salt and freshly ground
  black pepper

24 colossal or jumbo shrimp, heads-
  on and shell-on, deveined

Butter lettuce, for serving

Lime wedges, for serving

Fresh cilantro and mint leaves,
  for garnish

Preheat a gas or charcoal grill to medium-high heat (400°F to 450°F/205°C to 230°C) and lightly oil the grates.

While the grill heats, remove the shrimp from the marinade, draining off excess, and skewer them onto the skewers.

Lay the shrimp directly on the grill (if using charcoal) and cook for 2 to 3 minutes. Then flip and cook on the other side for another 2 to 3 minutes, until the shrimp are cooked through and the edges have a nice char to them.

Remove the shrimp to a platter and and serve alongside the butter lettuce, lime wedges, and herbs as a DIY lettuce wrap. Remove the shell from the shrimp and place into a lettuce cup, drizzle with green goddess dressing, and top with quick pickled spicy carrots.

PRO TIP: If using wooden skewers, be sure to soak them in water for at least 30 minutes before use.

Grilled CLAMS with Garlic Breadcrumbs

PREP TIME: 10 minutes   **COOK TIME:** 15 minutes   **YIELD:** Serves 4 to 6

One of the best parts of cooking with shellfish is that it comes with its own built-in sauce: the ocean-y brine that's housed right in the shell. Normally we'd serve a clam dish with extra bread to sop up all that goodness, but this preparation builds that right into the recipe. The crispy, buttery breadcrumb topping soaks up all the juices that are released during cooking. And the major bonus is that you don't have to do any shucking because the heat of the grill will pop the clams open for you.

Preheat a gas or charcoal grill to high heat (450°F to 500°F/230°C to 260°C) and lightly oil the grates.

TO MAKE THE BREADCRUMBS: Melt the butter in the oil in a large skillet on the grill. Add the garlic and cook for 1 to 2 minutes, until translucent and fragrant. Stir in the breadcrumbs and cook, stirring often, for 2 to 3 minutes, until toasted. Turn off the heat, add the parsley, lemon zest, cheese, and salt. Transfer the mixture to a plate and set aside.

TO MAKE THE GARLIC BUTTER: In the same skillet, combine the butter and garlic and cook over medium heat until the butter is melted. Remove to a cool part of the grill or off the grill entirely.

TO GRILL THE CLAMS AND SERVE: Scatter the clams in a single layer across the grill. Close the grill and cook until the clams open, 6 to 10 minutes depending on size. As soon as they open, using tongs, transfer the clams to the skillet with the garlic butter. Toss to combine. Sprinkle with the reserved breadcrumbs, and then transfer to a serving platter or bowls. Garnish with parsley and serve with lemon wedges.

FOR THE BREADCRUMBS:
4½ teaspoons unsalted butter
1½ teaspoons olive oil
2 cloves garlic, minced
½ cup (40 g) panko breadcrumbs
2 tablespoons chopped fresh parsley
Zest of ½ lemon
2 tablespoons freshly grated
  Parmesan cheese
⅛ teaspoon kosher salt

FOR THE GARLIC BUTTER:
½ cup (115 g/1 stick) unsalted butter
1 tablespoon minced garlic

FOR THE GRILLED CLAMS:
24 littleneck clams, scrubbed
Chopped fresh parsley, for garnish
Lemon wedges, for serving

Spicy
WHOLE GRILLED FISH with Avocado Salad

PREP TIME: 15 minutes   **COOK TIME:** 10 minutes   **YIELD:** Serves 4

Branzino sounds fancy, looks fancy, and tastes fancy, but I assure you, cooking it is anything but fancy. Ask your butcher to clean the fish for you (it should be gutted and scaled), so all you need to do is give it a dip in a dreamy coconut cream marinade with plenty of green chile heat, then pop it onto the grill. I love serving this with a quick avocado salad to tame the heat and provide a little texture with your tender, flaky fish.

FOR THE DRESSING:

1 tablespoon fresh lemon juice

2 teaspoons red wine vinegar

1 shallot, minced

⅓ cup (70 ml) olive oil

Kosher salt and freshly ground
    black pepper

FOR THE FISH:

½ cup (26 g) chopped yellow onion

4 cloves garlic, peeled

1 serrano chile, stemmed

1 tablespoon grated fresh ginger

¼ cup (60 ml) fresh lime juice

2 tablespoons neutral oil,
    such as avocado or grapeseed

3 tablespoons unsweetened
    coconut cream

1 teaspoon ground cumin

1 teaspoon ground coriander

1 teaspoon honey

1 bunch cilantro, roughly chopped,
    plus torn leaves for garnish

1 teaspoon kosher salt

4 whole fish (1¼ pounds/568 g
    each), such as branzino or rainbow
    trout, gutted and scales removed

3 heads Little Gem lettuce,
    torn into individual leaves,
    ends trimmed and cleaned

2 avocados, cut into large dice

Lime wedges, for serving

TO MAKE THE DRESSING: Combine the lemon juice, vinegar, and shallots in a serving bowl and whisk in the oil. Season with salt and pepper. Set aside until it's time to serve the salad.

Preheat a gas or charcoal grill to medium-high heat (400°F to 450°F/205°C to 230°C) and lightly oil the grates.

TO MARINATE THE FISH: Combine the onion, garlic, chile, ginger, lime juice, oil, coconut cream, cumin, coriander, honey, cilantro, and salt in a blender and blend until smooth.

Rinse the fish inside and out and pat dry. With a sharp knife, cut 3 deep slices on each side of the fish and season lightly with salt and pepper. Place the fish in a baking dish and cover with the sauce.

Place the fish on the grill, close the lid, and cook for about 5 minutes without disturbing the fish. Use a fish spatula and tongs to carefully flip the fish and cook for an additional 4 to 5 minutes, until it is 145°F (63°C) in the thickest part of the fish. Remove from the grill to a platter.

To serve, add the lettuce and avocado to the dressing in the bowl. Season with salt and pepper and toss to coat. Divide the salad and fish among four plates. Garnish with torn cilantro leaves and serve with lime wedges.

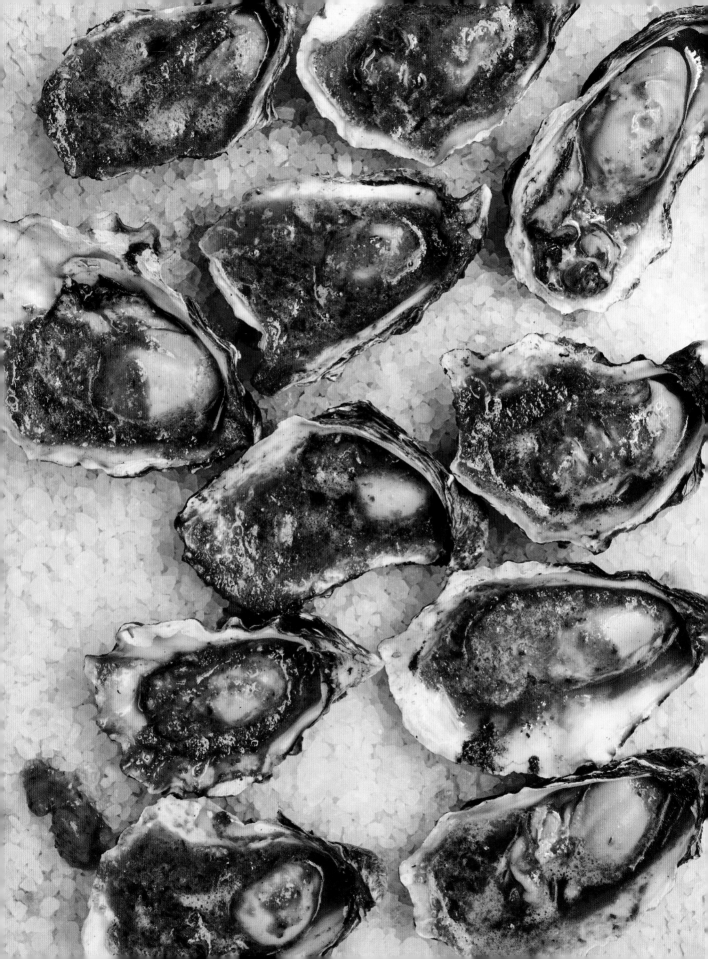

Grilled
OYSTERS

PREP TIME: 20 minutes   **COOK TIME:** 5 minutes   **YIELD:** Serves 4

The entire WGC team is obsessed with grilled oysters. If they're on a menu, we're ordering them. Don't get me wrong, this girl will take down a dozen icy cold ones any day, but when they're all smoky from the grill and topped with flavored butter? Heaven. It's such a fun and sophisticated starter to throw into your entertaining mix. Serve with Champagne, if you're feeling extra.

Combine the softened butter, brown sugar, garlic, chipotles, adobo sauce, lime juice, salt, and pepper in the bowl of a small food processor and process until smooth. Remove the butter mixture to a resealable container and refrigerate it until hardened. (You can make the butter up to 2 weeks in advance.) Feel free to use excess butter on toasted bread, or drizzled on vegetables or any other fish.

Preheat a gas or charcoal grill to medium-high heat (400°F to 450°F/205°C to 230°C) and lightly oil the grates.

Place the freshly shucked oysters on a tray. Run a knife under each oyster to make sure the meat is released from the shell. Remove any bits of shell from inside the shell or on the oyster and put a rounded teaspoon of the butter mixture on each oyster.

Carefully move the oysters with the butter directly onto the grill. Cook for 3 to 5 minutes, until the butter is melted and begins to boil in the shell, taking care not to overcook.

Remove the oysters from the grill, let cool slightly, and serve with a squeeze of lime.

- 1 cup (230g/2 sticks) unsalted butter, softened
- ¼ cup (55 g) packed light brown sugar
- 8 cloves garlic, minced
- 4 canned chipotle chiles in adobo, minced
- 2 tablespoons adobo sauce (from the can of chipotles)
- 2 tablespoons fresh lime juice
- ½ teaspoon kosher salt
- ¼ teaspoon freshly ground black pepper
- 1 dozen medium-large oysters, freshly shucked
- Lime wedges, for serving

Buttery Herb
SCALLOP SKEWERS

PREP TIME: 10 minutes   **COOK TIME:** 10 minutes   **YIELD:** Serves 6

Here's the deal with scallops: They are delish any way you cook them, and they are much easier to make than most people think. The beauty of grilling them is that it makes the process that much simpler—just a quick hit of heat to develop those nice grill marks for that perfect caramelized crust, then a slather of herby butter to finish things off. If you're like me, serve these with pasta and an extra knob of the compound butter.

SPECIAL EQUIPMENT:

6 metal or wooden skewers

½ cup (115 g/1 stick) unsalted butter

4 cloves garlic, grated

Zest and juice of 1 lemon

2 tablespoons chopped fresh chives

2 tablespoons chopped fresh dill

2 tablespoons chopped fresh parsley

½ teaspoon kosher salt,
  plus more for the scallops

¼ teaspoon freshly ground black
  pepper, plus more for the scallops

24 large scallops

¼ cup (60 ml) olive oil

Preheat a gas or charcoal grill to medium heat (350°F to 400°F/175°C to 204°C) and lightly oil the grates.

Melt the butter in a small saucepan over medium heat. Add the garlic and cook, stirring frequently, until it is fragrant, 30 seconds to 1 minute. Remove the butter from the heat and add the lemon zest, lemon juice, chives, dill, parsley, salt, and pepper. Stir to combine.

Thread 4 scallops onto each skewer. Drizzle the scallops with the oil and season with salt and pepper. Transfer the scallops to the grill and cook for 3 to 4 minutes, until nice grill marks form. Flip the scallops and baste the grilled side with the herb butter. Cook for an additional 3 to 4 minutes, until the scallops are cooked through.

Remove the scallops to a serving platter and baste again with the herb butter. Serve with the remaining herb butter.

PRO TIP: If using wooden skewers, be sure to soak them in water for at least 30 minutes before use.

Grilled
MISO COD

PREP TIME: 10 minutes   **MARINATING TIME:** 24 hours   **COOK TIME:** 10 minutes   **YIELD:** Serves 4

I used to make this dish once a week when I was a private chef, and I will forever be a fan of it. (Much gratitude to Nobu Matsuhisa for starting the miso cod craze!) It gets a rich, complex, sweet-savory flavor from just a few ingredients, and with a little bit of prep time, you'll have a restaurant-worthy meal to make any weeknight feel fancy.

To make the marinade, combine the sake and mirin in a small saucepan and bring to a boil over medium-high heat. Let the mixture boil for a minute or so, until the harsh alcohol smell burns off. Turn the heat down to low and add the miso paste and sugar. Gently whisk until the miso is incorporated and the sugar has dissolved. Remove from the heat and let cool to room temperature before continuing.

Pat the fish dry and place it in a glass baking dish or zip-top bag. Cover the fish with the marinade and refrigerate for 24 hours.

Preheat a gas or charcoal grill to medium heat (350°F to 400°F/175°C to 204°C) and lightly oil the grates.

Remove the fish from the marinade and blot with paper towels to remove excess marinade. Lightly brush the flesh with oil and transfer the fillets to the grill flesh-side down. Lightly brush the skin with oil. Cook for 3 to 5 minutes, until nice grill marks form and the fish easily releases from the grill. Flip and cook for an additional 3 to 5 minutes, until the skin is crisp and the fish flakes easily with a fork. Remove from the grill and serve immediately.

¼ cup (60 ml) sake

¼ cup (60 ml) mirin

¼ cup (60 ml) white miso paste

2 tablespoons granulated sugar

4 (6- to 8-ounce/170 to 225 g) skin-on black cod fillets

Neutral oil, such as avocado or grapeseed

NOTE: If you're nervous about cooking the fish directly on the grill grates, feel free to use a plancha. If you do go for the grates, be sure to oil them really well (see page 14) and don't try to flip the fish before it naturally releases from the grill.

PIZZA.

BURGERS
Necessary
OTHER CARBS

If you've been a part of the WGC community for any amount of time, then you know that pizza and burgers are my love language. And the only thing more on-brand than carbs on carbs with meat and cheese and veg is grilling up all that goodness. Adding a wood-burning pizza oven to our outdoor cooking set-up has been such a game-changer for us because Thomas and I can whip up some seriously legit pies in minutes. Well, as it turns out, you can do the exact same thing on your grill with the help of a pizza stone. We're talking soft, chewy crust with just the right amount of char and all your favorite ingredients—plus a few new ones. As for burgers (and brats), it just wouldn't be a proper grilling book without teaching you how to make the juiciest, cheesiest, boldest, baddest sandwiches of all time. I think it's safe to say that you're about to be looking forward to dinners at home a lot more than usual.

The PIZZA GRILLING *Commandments*

1.

DON'T OVERLOAD YOUR TOPPINGS.

You'll end up with a soggy-bottom pie, and no
one wants anything to do with a soggy bottom.

2.

WHEN DISTRIBUTING YOUR TOPPINGS,

keep them lighter toward the center of
the pie and heavier toward the crust, which is
the sturdiest part of the pizza.

3.

NO NEED TO BUY PIZZA SAUCE.

Get a can of pureed San Marzano tomatoes,
add a pinch of salt, and you're good to go.
Use leftovers for pasta.

Grilled Spicy
DIAVOLO PIZZA

PREP TIME: 10 minutes   **COOK TIME:** 10 minutes   **YIELD:** Serves 4 to 6

Consider this your major pepperoni pizza upgrade. Soppressata is like pepperoni's more sophisticated Southern Italian cousin who still brings that great spiced flavor but a little more polish. And because the soppressata is sliced so thin, you can ignore the Pizza Commandments and get crazy here—the more cured meat the better. Add a cheese blend and some salty, briny olives to the mix, and you're never going to order takeout again.

Flour, for work surface

1 pound (455 g) pizza dough

Olive oil, for brushing

½ cup (120 ml) tomato sauce

1 to 2 cups (110 to 220 g) Tillamook Farmstyle Whole-Milk Mozzarella cheese shreds

Thinly sliced soppressata

½ cup (200 g) crushed pitted Castelvetrano olives

Kosher salt and freshly ground black pepper

GARNISHES:

Fresh basil leaves

Parmesan flakes

Olive oil

Red pepper flakes

Preheat a gas or charcoal grill to high heat (450°F to 500°F/230°C to 260°C) and lightly oil the grates.

Lightly flour a clean work surface and rimless baking sheet or pizza peel. On your work surface, shape the dough into 2 medium-ish pizzas. Let the dough sit for 5 minutes, then re-form it as big as you'd like. One at a time, place the pizza dough on the prepared baking sheet or pizza peel. Lightly brush both sides of the pizza with oil to prevent sticking to the grill.

Slide the pizza dough directly onto the grill, close the lid, and grill for about 2 minutes, until grill marks appear on the bottom. Using tongs, lift the lid, flip the dough, close the lid again, and cook for about 2 minutes more, until the dough is golden brown with grill marks on both sides.

Remove the dough from the grill and place it back on the baking sheet. Reduce the heat on the grill to medium (350°F to 400°F/175°C to 204°C).

Carefully spread the tomato sauce on top of each pizza, leaving a bit of room for the crust. Divide the cheese, soppressata, and olives between the pizzas. Carefully transfer the pizzas one at a time back to the grill and cover to melt the cheese.

Using tongs, remove the pizzas from the grill and season with salt and pepper. Add your desired garnishes, slice, and serve.

Grilled
SALAD PIZZA

PREP TIME: 10 minutes **COOK TIME:** 10 minutes **YIELD:** Serves 4 to 6

A salad that just so happens to have a pizza crust beneath it is really just a salad, right? So the way I see it, we all need to be doing ourselves a favor and eating way more salad pizzas. You'll be amazed at what happens when the lettuce hits the heat with the tomatoes, provolone, and pepperoncinis—it's the most delicious self-care you'll ever have.

Preheat a gas or charcoal grill to high heat (450°F to 500°F/230°C to 260°C) and lightly oil the grates.

Lightly flour a clean work surface and rimless baking sheet or pizza peel. On your work surface, shape the dough into 2 medium-ish pizzas. Let the dough sit for 5 minutes, then re-form it as big as you'd like. One at a time, place the pizza dough on the prepared baking sheet or pizza peel. Lightly brush both sides of the pizza with oil to prevent sticking to the grill.

Slide the pizza dough directly onto the grill, close the lid, and grill for about 2 minutes, until grill marks appear on the bottom. Using tongs, lift the lid, flip the dough, close the lid again, and cook for about 2 minutes more, until the dough is golden brown with grill marks on both sides.

Remove the dough from the grill and place it back on the baking sheet. Reduce the heat on the grill to medium (350°F to 400°F/175°C to 204°C).

Carefully spread the tomato sauce on top of each pizza, leaving a bit of room for the crust. Divide the cheese and red onion between the pizzas. Carefully transfer the pizzas one at a time back to the grill and cover to melt the cheese.

Using tongs, remove the pizzas from the grill and season with salt and pepper. Add your desired garnishes, slice, and serve.

Flour, for work surface

1 pound (455 g) pizza dough

Olive oil, for brushing

½ cup (120 ml) store-bought yellow tomato sauce

2 cups (220 g) shredded provolone cheese

¼ cup (60 g) super thinly sliced red onion

Kosher salt and freshly ground black pepper

GARNISHES:

⅔ cup (100 g) Sungold tomatoes

½ cup (74 g) sliced pepperoncinis

1 to 2 heads Little Gem lettuce, leaves separated, cleaned, and tossed with 1 to 2 tablespoons red wine vinegar or lemon juice

4 to 6 ounces (115 to 170 g) soppressata

Grilled Calabrian
CHEESE PIZZA

PREP TIME: 10 minutes **COOK TIME:** 10 minutes **YIELD:** Serves 4 to 6

When I "discovered" jarred Calabrian chiles a few years ago, I couldn't resist adding them to anything and everything because their sweet heat makes any dish better, and everyone knows that dribbles of bright red oil is the universal sign for tasty. The chiles bring this simple ricotta and basil pizza together into one very complete, very delicious thought.

Flour, for work surface

1 pound (455 g) pizza dough

⅓ cup (71 g) olive oil, plus more for brushing

6 cloves garlic, finely chopped

⅓ cup (37 g) shredded provolone cheese

⅔ cup (75 g) Tillamook Farm-style Triple Cheddar Blend cheese shreds

⅓ cup (83 g) whole-milk ricotta cheese

Kosher salt and freshly ground black pepper

GARNISHES:

Calabrian chiles in oil

Fresh basil leaves

Preheat a gas or charcoal grill to high heat (450°F to 500°F/230°C to 260°C) and lightly oil the grates.

Lightly flour a clean work surface and rimless baking sheet or pizza peel. On your work surface, shape the dough into 2 medium-ish pizzas. Let the dough sit for 5 minutes, then re-form it as big as you'd like. One at a time, place the pizza dough on the prepared baking sheet or pizza peel. Lightly brush both sides of the pizza with oil to prevent sticking to the grill.

Slide the pizza dough directly onto the grill, close the lid, and grill for about 2 minutes, until grill marks appear on the bottom. Using tongs, lift the lid, flip the dough, close the lid again, and cook for about 2 minutes more, until the dough is golden brown with grill marks on both sides.

Remove the dough from the grill and place it back on the baking sheet. Reduce the heat on the grill to medium (350°°F to 400°F/175°°C to 204°C).

Carefully spread the olive oil and garlic on top of the pizzas, leaving a bit of room for the crust. Divide the cheeses between the pizzas. Carefully transfer the pizzas one at a time back to the grill and cover to melt the cheese.

Using tongs, remove the pizzas from the grill and season with salt and pepper. Add your desired garnishes, slice, and serve.

Grilled Oregano
WHITE PIZZA

PREP TIME: 10 minutes   **COOK TIME:** 10 minutes   **YIELD:** Serves 4 to 6

OK, I'm taking some liberties in calling this a white pizza because technically it has a little sauce, but the main attraction of this pie is the layers of fresh and smoked mozzarella, garlic, basil, and oregano, which add up to the perfect white(ish) pie experience. No matter what you call it, it's giving serious spritz and headscarf vibes à la the Amalfi Coast.

Preheat a gas or charcoal grill to high heat (450°F to 500°F/230°C to 260°C) and lightly oil the grates.

Lightly flour a clean work surface and rimless baking sheet or pizza peel. On your work surface, shape the dough into 2 medium-ish pizzas. Let the dough sit for 5 minutes, then re-form it as big as you'd like. One at a time, place the pizza dough on the prepared baking sheet or pizza peel. Lightly brush both sides of the pizza with oil to prevent sticking to the grill.

Slide the pizza dough directly onto the grill, close the lid, and grill for about 2 minutes, until grill marks appear on the bottom. Using tongs, lift the lid, flip the dough, close the lid again, and cook for about 2 minutes more, until the dough is golden brown with grill marks on both sides.

Remove the dough from the grill and place it back on the baking sheet. Reduce the heat on the grill to medium (350°F to 400°F/175°C to 204°C).

Mix together the olive oil, tomato sauce, garlic, and dried oregano in a medium bowl. Carefully spread the sauce on top of each pizza, leaving a bit of room for the crust. Divide the cheeses between the pizzas. Carefully transfer the pizzas one at a time back to the grill and cover to melt the cheese.

Using tongs, remove the pizzas from the grill and season with salt and pepper. Add your desired garnishes, slice, and serve.

Flour, for work surface

1 pound (455 g) pizza dough

¼ cup (60 ml) olive oil, plus more for brushing

¼ cup (60 ml) tomato sauce

8 cloves garlic, finely minced

1 teaspoon dried oregano

1 cup (150 g) torn fresh mozzarella cheese

1 cup (110 g) shredded smoked mozzarella cheese

Kosher salt and freshly ground black pepper

GARNISHES:

Fresh basil leaves

Fresh oregano leaves

Grilled
BEER BRATS

PREP TIME: 10 minutes   **COOK TIME:** 20 minutes   **YIELD:** Serves 4 to 6

I'm German, which means that bratwursts and beer are in my DNA. A traditional preparation is to braise these spiced pork sausages in beer with loads of onions, and I see no reason to mess with tradition. Bundle it all up in a bun, dress it with whatever toppings you like—ketchup, mustard, BBQ sauce—and call it a successful weekend afternoon.

1 pound (455 g) bratwurst
(4 to 6 sausages)

1 medium yellow onion, thinly sliced

2 teaspoons red pepper flakes

1 teaspoon garlic powder

1 teaspoon kosher salt

½ teaspoon freshly ground
black pepper

24 ounces (710 ml) beer of choice

Brioche hot dog buns, toasted

Ketchup, mustard, or BBQ sauce,
for serving

Prepare your grill for zone grilling, with a zone of direct high heat (450°F to 500°F/230°C to 260°C) and a zone of direct low heat (250°F to 350°F/120°C to 175°C). If using a gas grill, begin preheating at least 15 minutes prior to grilling. If using charcoal, light the charcoal at least 30 minutes prior to grilling.

Put the brats, onion, red pepper flakes, garlic powder, salt, pepper, and beer in a large cast-iron skillet and place directly on the grill grates over the low heat zone. Close the grill. Bring to a boil and cook for 10 to 12 minutes, until the brats reach about 145°F (63°C).

Use grill tongs to carefully transfer the beer-boiled brats directly to the grill grates over the high heat zone, shaking off any excess liquid. (Keep the skillet on the low heat zone.) Grill the brats for 2 to 3 minutes per side, until charred as desired and the internal temperature reaches 160°F (71°C). Let the brats rest for a few minutes before serving.

Serve the brats on toasted buns topped with the beer-braised onions and your favorite toppings—I'm a ketchup gal, but everyone else in my life is Team Mustard. Do what makes you happy.

Grilled
NACHOS
with Chipotle-Crusted Steak

PREP TIME: 30 minutes   **MARINATING TIME:** 30 minutes   **COOK TIME:** 20 minutes   **YIELD:** Serves 4

It always surprises people when I tell them that steak can be an ideal cut of meat to feed a big group. Cuts like skirt steak, flank steak, and hanger steak are best served sliced, so you're getting more mileage from one steak; they're inexpensive; and they're really versatile. You could of course serve them next to any of the veggies or sides recipes in this book and have a solid meal, or you could take a page from my go-to lazy girl entertaining menu/Sunday dinner and scatter the slices over these loaded grilled nachos along with some grilled tomatillo salsa and never look back. Just don't forget to use my patented No Naked Chip™ technique and coat each and every one with plenty of cheese.

Preheat a gas or charcoal grill to medium-high heat (400°F to 450°F/205°C to 230°C) and lightly oil the grates.

Sprinkle the steak on both sides with salt, pepper, and 1 teaspoon of the chipotle chile powder. In an 11 × 7-inch (28 × 18 cm) glass dish, whisk 1½ tablespoons of the oil and 1 tablespoon of the lime juice. Add the meat and turn to coat. Cover and marinate at room temperature for 30 minutes.

Meanwhile, brush the corn with 1 tablespoon of the remaining oil and sprinkle with salt and pepper. Grill the corn for 7 minutes, or until slightly charred, turning occasionally. Cut the corn from the cob and transfer the kernels to a bowl. Stir in the cilantro, chives, lime zest, and remaining ¼ teaspoon chipotle powder, ½ tablespoon oil, and 1 tablespoon lime juice. Season with salt and pepper.

Grill the steak to desired doneless: for skirt steak, about 2½ minutes per side for medium; for flank, it's 4 to 5 minutes per side; for hanger, follow the directions on page 24. Transfer to a cutting board and let rest for 5 minutes. Slice the steak across the grain, then chop into small bite-size pieces.

Arrange the tortilla chips in an even layer on a baking sheet. Add a spoonful of salsa to each chip, followed by an aggressive amount of the shredded cheeses, the chopped steak, and corn.

Reduce the grill to medium-low heat and transfer the baking sheet onto the grill over indirect heat, cover, and cook for 5 to 10 minutes, until the cheese is fully melted. Remove from the grill and serve with guacamole.

8 ounces (225 g) skirt or flank steak (or leftover hanger steak; see page 24)

Kosher salt and freshly ground black pepper

1¼ teaspoons chipotle chile powder, divided

3 tablespoons olive oil, divided

2 tablespoons fresh lime juice, divided (from 1 lime, zest reserved)

2 ears corn, shucked

¼ cup (10 g) chopped fresh cilantro

2 tablespoons chopped fresh chives

16 Corn Tortilla Chips (recipe follows)

1 cup (240 ml) Salsa Verde (recipe follows)

1 cup (110 g) Tillamook Farmstyle Medium Cheddar cheese shreds

1 cup (110 g) Tillamook Monterey Jack cheese shreds

Guacamole (page 228)

(recipe continues)

CORN TORTILLA CHIPS

PREP TIME: 1 minute
COOK TIME: 2 minutes
YIELD: 20 chips

½ cup (120 ml) vegetable oil
5 small corn tortillas, cut into quarters

Juice of 1 lime
1 teaspoon kosher salt

In a large heavy-bottomed pan over high heat, add the oil. Once the oil is shimmering, add a few of the tortilla triangles at a time and fry for about 1 minute on each side, until crisp. Remove from the oil and transfer to a paper towel–lined plate. Sprinkle with a few drops of the lime juice as they cool and finish with salt.

SALSA VERDE

PREP TIME: 10 minutes
COOK TIME: 10 minutes
YIELD: Makes 1½ to 2 cups (360 to 480 ml)

1 pound (455 g) tomatillos, papery husk discarded
1 jalapeño chile, stemmed
1 small white onion, peeled and cut into ⅓-inch (8 mm) rounds
2 tablespoons olive oil

Kosher salt and freshly ground black pepper
2 cloves garlic, smashed and peeled
½ cup (30 g) tightly packed fresh cilantro leaves
Juice of 2 limes

Preheat a gas or charcoal grill to medium-high heat (400°F to 450°F/205°C to 230°C) and lightly oil the grates.

Combine the tomatillos, jalapeño, and onions in a large bowl and drizzle with the oil and a generous pinch of salt and pepper.

Add the tomatillos, jalapeño, and onions to the grill (you can use a grill basket). Cook, turning occasionally, 5 to 10 minutes, until the tomatillos are softened and the jalapeño and onions are charred. Remove the vegetables to a plate and let cool slightly.

Transfer the vegetables, garlic, cilantro, and lime juice to a blender and blend on high speed until smooth. Season with salt and pepper. Store in an airtight container for up to 10 days.

Lemongrass
BURGERS with Spicy Napa Slaw

PREP TIME: 20 minutes   **COOK TIME:** 8 minutes   **YIELD:** Serves 4

Up until now, you may have only seen lemongrass in Thai curries, but it's traditional in Vietnamese cooking to pair it with beef. So we're going back to Southeast Asia for this slaw-mounded, spicy mayo–slathered burger, which gets tons of bold, bright flavor from soy, ginger, lime, and plenty of chiles.

FOR THE SLAW:

2 cups (180 g) thinly sliced
   napa cabbage

1 cup (50 g) julienned carrots

1 to 2 jalapeño chiles, thinly sliced

2 tablespoons chopped fresh cilantro

2 tablespoons toasted sesame oil

2 tablespoons rice vinegar

1 tablespoon honey

1 tablespoon soy sauce

2 teaspoons grated fresh ginger

2 teaspoons fresh lime juice

1 teaspoon sriracha

¼ teaspoon kosher salt

1 tablespoon sesame seeds

FOR THE BURGERS:

1 pound (455 g) ground beef

2 tablespoons minced lemongrass

1 tablespoon chopped fresh cilantro

2 teaspoons minced garlic

2 teaspoons soy sauce

1 teaspoon minced fresh ginger

1 teaspoon fish sauce

1 teaspoon light brown sugar

1 teaspoon toasted sesame oil

Kosher salt and freshly ground
   black pepper

2 tablespoons olive oil

4 tablespoons butter, softened

4 brioche buns

Spicy Mayo (page 228)

TO MAKE THE SLAW: Combine the cabbage, carrots, jalapeños, and cilantro in a large bowl. Whisk together the sesame oil, vinegar, honey, soy sauce, ginger, lime juice, sriracha, and salt in a small bowl. Taste and season with more salt as needed. Pour the dressing over the cabbage mixture and toss to coat well. Sprinkle the sesame seeds over the slaw, cover, and refrigerate until ready to serve.

Preheat a gas or charcoal grill to medium-high heat (400°F to 450°F/205°C to 230°C) and lightly oil the grates.

TO MAKE THE BURGERS: Mix together the ground beef, lemongrass, cilantro, garlic, soy sauce, ginger, fish sauce, brown sugar, and sesame oil in a large bowl. Season with salt and pepper. Form the mixture into 4 equal-size patties and drizzle with the olive oil.

Place the patties on the grill and cook for 3 to 4 minutes per side, until they are cooked to your desired doneness.

During the last few minutes of cooking, butter the brioche buns and place on the grill to lightly toast them.

Serve the hamburgers on the toasted buns slathered with spicy mayo and topped with the slaw.

Smashed
BUTTER BURGERS

PREP TIME: 20 minutes   **COOK TIME:** 10 minutes   **YIELD:** Serves 4

This is basically your classic backyard cookout burger. Except instead of an overcooked, dried-out patty, we're going for full-on juice factor. Am I grating a stick of butter into ground beef to make the patties? You bet your ass I am. And I've never been less sorry in my life. They're salty and fatty and I love them with my whole heart. Be prepared—this is over-the-top decadence.

Using a box grater, grate the frozen stick of butter on the smallest size holes. Combine the beef, grated butter, salt, pepper, and garlic powder in a large bowl. Don't overmix. Divide into 8 portions and loosely form into balls, about 4 ounces (113 g) for each. Cover with plastic wrap and set aside.

Preheat a gas or charcoal grill to high heat (450°F to 500°F/230°C to 260°C) with a cast-iron griddle on it. You want it smoking hot.

Split the buns and slather with mayonnaise on each cut side.

Toast the burger buns on the hot griddle for 1 to 2 minutes, until golden, making sure not to burn them. Remove from the heat.

Working quickly, place 4 of the burger balls on the griddle on the grill and, using a piece of parchment paper just bigger than the final patty size and a spatula, smash the ball into a thin burger. You want to really put some weight into it to make it as thin as possible. You can even use another metal spatula to assist in the smash. Slide the spatula off (don't pull it up). This will help the patty stay flat against the griddle.

Cook for 3 to 4 minutes; at the end, add a few slices of onion, then quickly flip the patties and give them another smash with the spatula. (Some cooks baste the patties with yellow mustard before the flip, but if you know me, you know how I feel about mustard.) Top each patty with sliced cheese, close the lid on the grill, and cook another 3 to 4 minutes, until the cheese is melted.

Stack 2 patties and place them on the bottom bun. Top with desired toppings and the top bun.

SPECIAL EQUIPMENT:

Cast-iron or grill-safe griddle

Flat, wide metal spatulas

½ cup (115 g/1 stick) unsalted butter, frozen

2 pounds (910 g) ground beef (80/20)

½ teaspoon kosher salt

½ teaspoon freshly ground black pepper

¼ teaspoon garlic powder

4 soft hamburger buns

4 tablespoons mayonnaise

1 large yellow onion, very thinly sliced

8 slices Tillamook Medium Cheddar

TOPPINGS:

Mayonnaise

Mustard

Ketchup

Shredded lettuce

Sliced tomatoes

Homemade Pickles (and Other Vegetables) (page 226)

Special Sauce (page 230)

Caramelized Onions (page 226)

Lamb
BURGERS with Whipped Feta and Grilled Cherry Tomatoes

PREP TIME: 10 minutes **COOK TIME:** 15 minutes **YIELD:** Serves 4

If you've ever had lamb kofta kebabs, then you know how this rich, fatty meat is perfect for grinding up into patties and cooking over fire. It seemed only right to supersize the situation into a cumin- and coriander-spiced burger and finish it off with a generous helping of garlicky, herby whipped feta for this Middle Eastern/Mediterranean dream of a burger.

SPECIAL EQUIPMENT:
4 metal or wooden skewers

FOR THE WHIPPED FETA:
1 (8-ounce/225 g) block feta cheese, halved
2 tablespoons (30 ml) sour cream
Zest and juice of ½ lemon
2 cloves garlic, minced
1 tablespoon chopped fresh dill
1 tablespoon chopped fresh parsley
Kosher salt and freshly ground black pepper, to taste

LAMB BURGERS:
1⅓ pounds (590 g) ground lamb
2 teaspoons chopped fresh oregano
2 teaspoons chopped fresh mint
3 cloves garlic, grated
½ teaspoon smoked paprika
1 teaspoon ground cumin
½ teaspoon ground coriander
¼ teaspoon ground cinnamon
½ teaspoon red pepper flakes
Kosher salt and freshly ground black pepper
2 cups (200 g) cherry tomatoes
¼ cup (60 ml) olive oil, plus more for brushing the rolls
1 teaspoon dried oregano
4 ciabatta rolls

TO MAKE THE WHIPPED FETA: Combine one-half of the feta, the sour cream, lemon zest, lemon juice, and garlic in a food processor and process until smooth. Crumble the remaining feta into the food professor and fold in along with the herbs, and salt and pepper and refrigerate until ready to serve.

Preheat a gas or charcoal grill to medium-high heat (400°F to 450°F/205°C to 230°C) and lightly oil the grates.

TO MAKE THE LAMB BURGERS: Put the ground lamb in a large bowl and break it up slightly with a fork. Add the fresh oregano, mint, garlic, smoked paprika, cumin, coriander, cinnamon, red pepper flakes, 1½ teaspoons salt, and ½ teaspoon pepper. Using clean hands, mix the meat so the spice mixture is evenly dispersed. Divide the meat mixture into 4 equal portions and form into patties. Place on a plate and set aside.

Combine the cherry tomatoes and oil in a medium bowl and season with salt, pepper, and the dried oregano. Thread the tomatoes onto the skewers. Skewering them helps prevent them from rolling around the grill while cooking (you could also use a grill basket to cook the tomatoes). As you assemble the skewers, set them on a baking sheet and set them aside until you're ready to grill. Slice the ciabatta rolls in half and lightly brush them with oil. Set aside.

Put the burger patties on the grill and cook about 4 minutes per side, or until the internal temperature is 145°F (63°C). Remove the patties from the grill and let rest while you grill the tomatoes and rolls.

Add the cherry tomatoes to the grill and cook for about 5 minutes, turning them, until charred in places and starting to burst. Add the ciabatta rolls to the grill and cook about 3 minutes, or until lightly charred and toasted. Remove the buns and tomatoes from the grill.

To assemble the burgers, add a patty to the bottom half of each roll. Top the patties with whipped feta, a few cherry tomatoes, and the top roll. Serve immediately.

PRO TIP: If using wooden skewers, be sure to soak them in water for at least 30 minutes before use.

Juicy LUCY

PREP TIME: 25 minutes   **COOK TIME:** 15 minutes   **YIELD:** Serves 4

If you haven't stuffed your hamburger patties with cheese, are you even living? This burger–Hot Pocket mash-up is the ultimate hack for nailing the juiciest, gooiest burgers every single time. Just don't skimp on the creamy "special sauce," which cuts some of the richness of the burger. But don't be fooled; this is nothing if not absolutely decadent. This might be the best recipe in the entire book. I said it.

Preheat a gas or charcoal grill to medium-high heat (400°F to 450°F/205°C to 230°C) and lightly oil the grates.

Put the ground beef, onion powder, garlic powder, salt, and pepper in a large bowl. Use clean hands to mix the meat mixture until evenly combined. Divide the mixture into 4 equal portions, then divide each portion in half, leaving you with 8 equal portions.

To form a burger, take one portion of beef and smash it into a round patty, slightly bigger than the bun. Take 1 slice of cheese and tear it into quarters. Shingle the cheese on the patty, leaving a ½-inch (1.25 cm) border. Take another portion of beef and flatten it to the same size as the first patty. Place it on top and gently crimp the patties together. Set the finished patty aside on a plate and continue the process with the remaining meat and cheese to make 4 patties total.

Put the burger patties on the grill and cook for 4 to 5 minutes per side, until the cheese is melted and gooey and the burger is cooked through. Remove the burger patties from the grill and let rest for 5 minutes.

While the burgers are resting, put the buns on the grill, cut-side down, and grill for 2 to 3 minutes, until lightly toasted.

To assemble the burgers, put a spoonful of sauce and a patty on each bottom bun. Top with your desired toppings and the top bun. Serve immediately.

1½ pounds (680 g) ground beef (80/20)
½ teaspoon onion powder
½ teaspoon garlic powder
1 heaping teaspoon kosher salt
½ teaspoon freshly ground black pepper
4 slices American cheese
4 potato buns
Special Sauce (page 230)

TOPPINGS:
Shredded iceberg lettuce
Sliced tomato
Sliced dill pickles

Dinner party:
SUMMER SEAFOOD

You know how big a fan I am of grilling seafood, so it seemed only right to team up some of my favorite seafood dishes to make one epic entirely grilled meal—down to the lemon s'mores pies. And, of course, you can't have a seafood feast without the perfect creamy coleslaw and an ice-cold tipsy Palmer.

Grilled
KING CRAB

PREP TIME: 20 minutes   **COOK TIME:** 12 minutes   **YIELD:** Serves 4

Preheat a gas or charcoal grill to medium-high heat (400°F to 450°F/205°C to 230°C) and lightly oil the grates.

Mix together the softened butter and lemon pepper in a small bowl and season with salt and pepper. Set aside at room temperature until ready to use.

Break the king crab at the knuckle and joints into smaller pieces. Use kitchen shears to split each piece of crab down the length of the interior white part of the crab. This allows easy access to the delicious meat. With a brush or your hands, coat the crab with the butter mixture, making sure to get some onto the meat. Pry the shell open a little if needed.

Once the grill is hot, transfer the crab to the grill, cover, and cook for 7 minutes, then flip the crab and continue to cook an additional 5 minutes.

Remove from the grill and sprinkle with lemon pepper, salt, and pepper. Serve with lemon wedges and the lemon pepper butter for dipping.

¼ cup (57 g/½ stick) unsalted butter, softened

2 teaspoons lemon pepper, plus more for serving

Kosher salt and freshly ground black pepper

4 pounds (1.8 kg) frozen king crab, thawed and rinsed

Lemon wedges, for serving

Low Country SHRIMP

PREP TIME: 25 minutes   **COOK TIME:** 20 minutes   **YIELD:** Serves 4 to 6

1 cup (230 g/2 sticks) unsalted butter, melted

6 to 8 cloves garlic, minced

3 tablespoons Old Bay Seasoning, divided, plus more for serving

3 ears corn, shucked and cut into pieces

14 ounces (400 g) smoked sausage, such as kielbasa, cut into pieces

1 pound (455 g) baby red potatoes, cut in half

1 lemon, quartered

2 tablespoons olive oil

2 pounds (910 g) jumbo shrimp, tails-on and shell-on, deveined

1 cup (240 ml) Pilsner-style beer or water

2 tablespoons snipped fresh chives

2 tablespoons chopped fresh parsley

Seafood Dipping Sauce (page 135)

Lemon wedges, for serving

Vinegar-based hot sauce, such as Tabasco, for serving

Preheat a gas or charcoal grill to medium-high heat (400°F to 450°F/205°C to 230°C) and lightly oil the grates.

Combine the melted butter, garlic, and 2 tablespoons of the Old Bay in a small bowl.

In a 9 × 13-inch (23 × 33 cm) grill-friendly baking pan or disposable aluminum pan, combine the corn, sausage, potatoes, and lemon quarters. Drizzle with the oil, sprinkle with the remaining 1 tablespoon Old Bay, and toss to combine. Let sit for 10 minutes.

Once the grill is hot, carefully place the corn, sausage, potatoes, and lemon quarters on the grill. Cook the lemon for 4 minutes, and the corn, sausage, and potatoes for 8 minutes, or until you see a nice char starting to develop.

Remove from the grill and place everything back into the baking pan. Top with the raw shrimp and drizzle with the melted garlic butter. Using tongs, toss to combine. Pour in the beer, cover tightly with foil, and place back on the grill. Close the lid, adjust the heat just below the pan to medium-low (350°F/175°C), and cook for 7 to 10 minutes, until cooked through.

Remove from the grill and take off the foil. Sprinkle with additional Old Bay, the chives, and parsley. Serve with seafood dipping sauce, lemon wedges, and hot sauce.

Seafood DIPPING SAUCE

PREP TIME: 5 minutes   **COOK TIME:** 13 minutes

Combine the onion, garlic, and water in a blender and blend until smooth.

Melt the butter in a medium skillet over medium-high heat. Add the onion and garlic mixture and cook for 5 minutes. Add the remaining ingredients and cook, stirring often, for another 5 to 8 minutes to blend the flavors. Remove from the heat and set aside to cool. Store in an airtight container in the fridge for up to 1 week.

1 small yellow onion, chopped

10 cloves garlic, chopped

½ cup (120 ml) water, beer, or chicken stock

1½ cups (340 g/3 sticks) unsalted butter

3 tablespoons Old Bay Seasoning

1 tablespoon smoked paprika

1½ teaspoons single-origin chile powder

1 teaspoon dried thyme

1 teaspoon ground ginger

1 teaspoon red pepper flakes

1 teaspoon freshly ground black pepper

1 teaspoon kosher salt

Zest and juice of 1 lemon

1 tablespoon vinegar-based hot sauce, such as Tabasco

3 tablespoons light brown sugar

Super Creamy COLESLAW

with a Kick

PREP TIME: 20 minutes **CHILLING TIME:** 1 to 6 hours **YIELD:** Serves 6

½ cup (120 ml) mayonnaise

¼ cup (60 ml) sour cream

1 tablespoon distilled white vinegar

1½ teaspoons apple cider vinegar

1 tablespoon granulated sugar

½ teaspoon celery seeds

Kosher salt and freshly ground black pepper

3 cups (300 g) finely shredded green cabbage

2 cups (200 g) finely shredded red cabbage

1 cup (150 g) finely shredded carrots

2 green onions, white and light green parts only, thinly sliced

1 jalapeño chile, cut in half, seeded, and thinly sliced

Whisk together the mayonnaise, sour cream, white vinegar, cider vinegar, sugar, and celery seeds in a large bowl. Season with salt and pepper.

Toss in both cabbages, the carrots, green onions, and jalapeño. Give it a good stir to make sure the dressing is evenly distributed. Cover and chill in the refrigerator for at least 1 hour or up to 6 hours before serving.

Batched
TIPSY PALMER

PREP TIME: 10 minutes **COOK TIME:** 5 minutes **STEEPING TIME:** 15 minutes
CHILLING TIME: 2 hours **YIELD:** Makes 8 drinks

TO MAKE THE LEMON SIMPLE SYRUP: Combine the water and sugar in a small saucepan and bring to a boil over medium heat. Add the lemon zest strips and remove from the heat. Let steep for 15 minutes, then remove the lemon zest, transfer the syrup to a container, and chill in the refrigerator at least 2 hours, until cold. The syrup will keep for up to 1 month.

TO MAKE THE PALMER: Pour the vodka, tea, lemon simple syrup, and lemon juice into a pitcher and stir to combine.

Serve over ice with lemon slices for garnish.

FOR THE LEMON SIMPLE SYRUP:
1 cup (240 ml) water
1 cup (200 g) granulated sugar
Zest of 2 lemons, removed with a peeler into long strips

FOR THE PALMER:
1½ cups (360 ml) vodka
2½ cups (600 ml) chilled unsweetened black tea
¾ cup (180 ml) lemon simple syrup (see above)
¾ cup (180 ml) fresh lemon juice

Ice
Lemon slices, for garnish

Lemon
S'MORES PIES

PREP TIME: 15 minutes   **CHILLING TIME:** 15 minutes   **COOLING TIME:** 3 to 12 hours   **YIELD:** Serves 8

SPECIAL EQUIPMENT:
8 (8-ounce/240 ml) Mason jars

FOR THE GRAHAM CRACKER LAYER:
1½ cups (180 g) crushed graham crackers
1½ tablespoons light brown sugar
9 tablespoons unsalted butter, melted

FOR THE LEMON LAYER:
6 large egg yolks
2 tablespoons grated lemon zest
2 (14-ounce/396 g) cans sweetened condensed milk
1 cup (240 ml) fresh lemon juice
1 teaspoon pure vanilla extract
Pinch of kosher salt

FOR THE WHITE CHOCOLATE GANACHE:
4 ounces (115 g) best-quality white chocolate, cut into small pieces
¼ cup (60 ml) heavy cream
1 tablespoon unsalted butter, at room temperature

2 cups (55 g) mini marshmallows
Broken graham crackers, for garnish

Preheat the oven to 350°F (175°C). Clean eight 8-ounce (240 ml) Mason jars.

TO MAKE THE GRAHAM CRACKER LAYER: Use a fork to mix the graham crackers, sugar, and butter in a small bowl until combined. Reserve about 8 tablespoons. Divide the remaining graham mixture among the 8 Mason jars—about 2 tablespoons each—pressing down lightly into the bottom.

TO MAKE THE LEMON LAYER: Combine the egg yolks and lemon zest in the bowl of a stand mixer fitted with the whisk attachment and beat on low speed for 2 to 3 minutes, until pale yellow and smooth. Mix in the sweetened condensed milk, lemon juice, vanilla, and salt with the machine on low until just combined.

Divide the lemon filling among the Mason jars. Place on a baking sheet and bake for about 15 minutes, until just set. Remove from the oven and let cool slightly, about 30 minutes.

TO MAKE THE WHITE CHOCOLATE GANACHE: When the pie jars are almost cool, put the chopped white chocolate in a small heatproof bowl. In a small saucepan over medium heat, bring the cream to a boil. Pour the cream over the chocolate and let sit for 45 seconds. Stir to combine and melt the white chocolate. When the mixture comes together, add the butter a little at a time and stir until combined and glossy. Let sit for 15 minutes.

Pour the ganache on top of the lemon layer, diving it equally among the Mason jars. Sprinkle on the reserved graham cracker mixture, about 1 tablespoon per jar. Cover with plastic wrap or the Mason jar lids and place in the refrigerator to chill for at least 3 hours and up to 12.

When ready to serve, top with mini marshmallows and carefully toast with a kitchen torch. (You can also brown the marshmallow topping in the oven. Place the marshmallow-topped jars back on a baking sheet and into the oven on the middle rack set to broil. Broil for 2 to 3 minutes. Keep an eye on it, as they will brown quickly.) Garnish with broken graham pieces.

GGIES

I've said it before, and I'll say it again: Grilling is not just for meat! It's one of THE best cooking methods for teasing out the best possible flavor and texture from veggies (and fruit, but that's another story for another chapter). Which means that a great side or main doesn't involve much more than seeing what looks good at the market, giving it a quick char, and loading it up with all manner of fresh herbs, cheeses, or any other of your favorite ingredients. The recipes in this chapter are your secret weapons for using up every last bit of great seasonal produce, actually looking forward to diving head-first into your veg, and nailing effortless chic when it comes to feeding guests.

Charred
PEPPERS with Whipped Feta

PREP TIME: 15 minutes   **COOK TIME:** 10 minutes   **YIELD:** Serves 6 to 8

For this Southwest-meets-SoCal lady, charred peppers are life. Grilling peppers brings out their natural sweetness and accentuates their natural smokiness, especially if you're using varieties like poblanos and shishitos. Slather some whipped feta over a platter, heap these peppers on top, and serve it as a side dish. Or add some grilled bread to make it more of an appetizer or snack-y situation. If you're using large peppers, cut out the cores and quarter the peppers; leave shishitos and Padróns whole.

3 pounds (1.4 kg) mixed peppers (red, orange, yellow, poblano, and shishito or Padróns)

¼ cup (60 ml) olive oil

2 tablespoons red wine vinegar

2 cloves garlic, chopped

½ teaspoon red pepper flakes

Kosher salt and freshly cracked black pepper

Whipped feta (see page 124)

Fresh basil leaves, for garnish

Fresh mint leaves, for garnish

Put the peppers on the grill and cook, turning occasionally, until blackened in spots and nearly cooked through, about 10 minutes (Padróns and shishitos may need less time). Let cool. You can remove the skin if you prefer (some of it will come off when you slice the peppers into strips). Cut into 1-inch-wide (2.5 cm) strips.

Place the peppers in a large bowl and toss with the oil, vinegar, garlic, and red pepper flakes. Season with salt and pepper. Slather the whipped feta on the bottom of a serving platter, arrange the peppers on top, and finish with the basil and mint.

LET'S TALK PEPPERS

Get creative! We all love bell peppers on the grill, but try using Padróns, shishitos, poblanos, Anaheims, and more. All peppers are super flavorful! Here are some tips:

1. USE HIGH HEAT. A good char is the key to flavorful peppers! Most of the skin will come off when you peel/slice, so not to worry if the outside becomes totally black.

2. DIRECT HEAT IS BEST! Unless you want them to take a long time to char, use high heat and let the peppers get in there and start to blister.

3. ROTATE. Turn the peppers with a pair of tongs every 3 minutes or so once the skin is charred until the entire pepper is uniformly charred.

4. BE PATIENT WHEN IT COMES TO PEELING. Once the peppers are charred, I like to seal them in a plastic bag or put them in a bowl and cover with plastic wrap to let them steam. This makes the skin even easier to peel off.

Grilled
BREAD SALAD with Mozzarella, Peaches, and Tomato

PREP TIME: 15 minutes   **COOK TIME:** 4 minutes   **YIELD:** Serves 4 to 6

Panzanella, or bits of bread teeming with olive oil and toasted, then tossed with tomatoes and vinaigrette, is the quintessential summer salad. I wanted to shake things up a bit by throwing stone fruit into the mix, namely because whenever stone fruit season rolls around, I can't be trusted to not bring home an obscene amount and end up having to use them in every single meal that week. But peaches are a natural pairing with tomatoes because they come into season at the same time and complement each other's tart sweetness, so this salad is the definition of winning all around.

Preheat a gas or charcoal grill to medium heat (350°F to 400°F/175°C to 204°C).

TO MAKE THE LEMON VINAIGRETTE: While the grill is heating up, whisk together all the ingredients in a medium bowl. Taste and adjust the salt and pepper as needed.

TO MAKE THE CROUTONS: Tear the ciabatta bread into 1- to 2-inch (2.5 to 5 cm) pieces. Place in a large bowl, drizzle with the oil, and toss to combine. Using a grill pan, or braving the grates, transfer to the grill and toast until the bread is crisp and just lightly golden, 2 to 4 minutes. Remove from the grill and sprinkle with salt. Set aside while you assemble the rest of the salad.

TO ASSEMBLE THE SALAD: Arrange the cherry tomatoes, tomato wedges, peaches, nectarines, torn croutons, and cheese in a large serving bowl. Top with basil leaves, season with sea salt and pepper, and drizzle with the lemon vinaigrette.

FOR THE LEMON VINAIGRETTE:
Juice of 1 lemon

3 tablespoons red wine vinegar

6 tablespoons olive oil

1 shallot, finely minced

2 cloves garlic, finely minced

Kosher salt and freshly cracked black pepper to taste

FOR THE TORN CROUTONS:
½ loaf ciabatta bread (about 8 ounces/225 g or 5 cups torn)

½ cup (120 ml) olive oil

Kosher salt

FOR THE SALAD:
2 cups (200 g) heirloom cherry tomatoes, halved

2 full-size heirloom tomatoes, cut into wedges

2 ripe peaches, pitted and cut into wedges

2 ripe nectarines, pitted and cut into wedges

2 (8-ounce/225 g) large balls fresh mozzarella cheese, torn into large pieces

Fresh basil leaves, for garnish

Flaky sea salt and freshly cracked black pepper

Grilled
CHIMI MUSHROOMS

PREP TIME: 10 minutes **COOK TIME:** 8 minutes **YIELD:** Serves 4 to 6

Mushrooms are the plant world's equivalent of a big, juicy steak. They have the same meaty texture and, when seasoned and cooked properly, can be just as satisfying. I know people love their portobello mushrooms, but I've never been a fan of the gills, so I started experimenting with all different varieties and fell in love with king trumpet, among other wild 'shrooms. Slice 'em in half, toss 'em on the grill for a hearty side dish, and then let 'em take a soak in a garlicky chimi marinade. Pro tip: For trumpet mushrooms, eat them flat-side down on your tongue. Don't ask me why, but they just taste better that way.

---

3 pounds (1.4 kg) wild mushrooms (trumpets are my favorite, but any large variety will work), torn or sliced

6 tablespoons olive oil

Kosher salt and freshly cracked black pepper

Calabrian Chimichurri (see page 38)

Fresh lemon juice

Preheat a gas or charcoal grill to medium heat (350°F to 400°F/175°C to 204°C).

Place the mushrooms in a large bowl and toss with the oil. Season with salt and pepper and let sit for a few minutes for the oil to absorb.

Place the mushrooms on the grill and cook for 3 to 4 minutes per side, until they are tender. Remove from the grill back to the bowl. Add the chimichurri and toss to coat. Taste and adjust the salt and pepper as needed. Finish with a squeeze of lemon.

Veggie
FRITTATA

PREP TIME: 10 minutes   **COOK TIME:** 25 minutes   **YIELD:** Serves 6 to 8

As I mentioned in the introduction, this is the dish that started it all. I needed a way to make one of life's greatest, most versatile, most user-friendly dishes, and it turned out that the grill was the way to go. Frittatas truly are a lifesaver—you only need a small handful of ingredients, they're hearty and filling, they're perfect for any meal, and you can stuff them full of pretty much anything. But what really takes them to the next level are some perfectly charred veg. Consider it your new signature dish for brunch, lunch, or dinner.

Set up a two-zone grill on your gas grill, one area over direct heat and one over indirect heat with the temperature of the grill roughly 400°F (205°C). Place a 10-inch (25 cm) cast-iron skillet on the direct heat side of the grill and let it warm up to medium-high heat.

Whisk together the eggs, cream, garlic, kosher salt, and pepper to taste in a large bowl until well combined. Set aside.

Add the oil to the cast-iron skillet on the grill. Add the shallot and cook about 5 minutes, or until translucent. Add the grilled peppers and spinach and cook until the spinach is wilted, then add the egg mixture, carefully stirring with a spatula to make sure everything is evenly incorporated. Move the skillet to the second zone for indirect heat.

Tuck the chunks of feta into the frittata and close the lid to the grill. Cook for 15 to 20 minutes, until the eggs are set. Carefully remove from the heat. Drizzle with oil, sprinkle with flaky sea salt, and serve.

8 large eggs

¼ cup (60 ml) heavy cream

2 cloves garlic, finely chopped

½ teaspoon kosher salt,
  plus more for sprinkling

Freshly ground black pepper

1½ teaspoons olive oil, plus more for
  drizzling

1 shallot, sliced

1½ cups (210 g) grilled bell peppers
  (see page 146), cut into 1-inch
  (2.5 cm) chunks

2 cups (60 g) fresh spinach leaves

¾ cup (115 g) feta cheese (the kind
  that comes in blocks in the brine),
  torn into large chunks

Flaky sea salt, for finishing

Cheddar Bacon
BBQ POTATOES

PREP TIME: 15 minutes   **COOK TIME:** 25 minutes   **YIELD:** Serves 4 to 6

This is a Bruce Dalkin specialty and the taste of my childhood. My dad is the king of foil packet potatoes, and while it may not be super chic, it's legit delish. It's also super versatile because you can either dress these up with your favorite condiments—Calabrian chimichurri (see page 38), BBQ sauce, ketchup, mustard—or even serve them as a main dish (fried egg on top, anyone?). And because everything is so nicely contained in foil, it makes cleanup so easy that you'll forgive the rustic ambiance. It's the best way to cook a ton of potatoes for a crowd.

6 large Yukon Gold potatoes, cut into ½-inch (1.25 cm) cubes

1 medium yellow onion, finely chopped

2 tablespoons olive oil

1 teaspoon garlic salt

½ teaspoon paprika

Kosher salt and freshly cracked black pepper

4 strips cooked bacon (I prefer applewood-smoked bacon)

1 cup (110 g) shredded sharp Cheddar cheese

Chopped fresh chives, for garnish

Preheat a gas or charcoal grill to high heat (450°F to 500°F/230°C to 260°C) and lightly oil the grates.

Toss together the potatoes, onion, oil, garlic salt, and paprika in a large bowl and season with salt and pepper. Break up the cooked bacon into small bits and toss into the potato mixture, making sure the bacon is evenly distributed.

Tear off 4 large sheets of aluminum foil, about 16 inches (41 cm) long each. Divide the potato mixture among the 4 sheets and fold the sides up on both ends to create securely wrapped parcels for the potatoes.

Place the 4 parcels on the grill, cover, and cook for about 10 minutes on each side, until fully cooked and fork-tender. When flipping the potato parcels, be sure to use a pair of tongs and a spatula so the parcels stay intact. Uncover, open up each of the parcels, and distribute the cheese over the potatoes. Cook for about 1 minute more to melt the cheese.

Carefully remove the potato parcels from the grill, garnish with chives, and serve.

Charred
CORN PASTA SALAD

PREP TIME: 15 minutes   **COOK TIME:** 20 to 25 minutes   **YIELD:** Serves 4 to 6

When corn is in season, you better believe that it is going to show up in pretty much everything I'm cooking because there's nothing better than all that peak-sun sweetness. And if we're talking summer veg, then it only makes sense to be talking grilling too. Tossing the corn onto the grill caramelizes its natural sugars and lends a smoky-sweet burst of flavor to this loaded pasta salad.

Preheat a gas or charcoal grill to high heat (450°F to 500°F/230°C to 260°C) and lightly oil the grates.

Brush the corn with the oil and place on the grill. Cook on all sides until medium charred, 6 to 10 minutes. Remove from the grill, season with salt, and set aside to cool.

Meanwhile, cook the pasta according to the package directions until al dente. Drain and transfer to a large bowl.

Once cool enough to handle, remove the kernels from the cob. Transfer the corn to the bowl with the pasta and add the cheese, green onions, cilantro, jalapeño, and garlic. Season with lime juice and chile powder to taste and toss again. Taste and adjust the salt, lime juice, and chile powder. Serve immediately.

4 ears corn, shucked

2 tablespoons olive oil

Kosher salt

10 ounces (280 g) orecchiette pasta

6 ounces (170 g) cotija cheese, finely crumbled (feta is a great substitute)

½ cup (40 g) thinly sliced green onions, green parts only

½ cup (14 g) fresh cilantro leaves, finely chopped

1 jalapeño chile, seeded and finely chopped

2 cloves garlic, minced

Fresh lime juice

Chile powder

Grilled
ARTICHOKES with Garlic Aioli

PREP TIME: 20 minutes   **MARINATING TIME:** 20 minutes   **COOK TIME:** 50 minutes   **YIELD:** Serves 3 or 4

I used to think there was no greater luxury than having a restaurant make me one of my favorite dishes—artichokes with aioli. But when I realized how easy it is to make it myself, and how much better I could make it when I finished off the artichokes on the grill, I've never looked back. It's the ultimate treat, whether you're making this for yourself on a Thursday night or for guests on a Saturday.

---

3 or 4 large artichokes

1 lemon, cut into quarters

2 bay leaves

¼ cup (60 ml) olive oil

3 tablespoons red wine vinegar

1 shallot, minced

1 teaspoon coriander seeds, lightly crushed

1 teaspoon chopped garlic

1 teaspoon grainy Dijon mustard

¼ teaspoon kosher salt, plus more if needed

¼ teaspoon freshly ground black pepper, plus more if needed

2 lemons, halved

Aioli 101 (page 232), for serving

To prep the artichokes, fill a large bowl with water and squeeze in half of the lemon quarters. Put the squeezed lemons into the water. Clean and trim the artichokes and cut in half. Remove the chokes and discard. Place the cleaned and trimmed artichokes in the lemon water to prevent browning.

Fill a large pot with a couple inches of water, the remaining lemon quarters, and the bay leaves. Set a steaming basket inside the pot; be sure that the water doesn't touch the bottom of the steaming basket. Bring to a boil over medium-high heat, then add as many artichoke halves as you can fit into the basket in a single layer. Steam the artichokes for 25 to 35 minutes, until you can easily pierce the hearts with a knife. If you didn't fit all the artichokes in the pot on the first round, do another round.

To make the vinaigrette, combine the olive oil, red wine vinegar, shallot, coriander seeds, garlic, Dijon, salt, and pepper in a small bowl and whisk together. Taste and adjust salt and pepper as needed.

Place the artichokes in the bowl with the vinaigrette and toss to coat. Let marinate for 15 to 20 minutes on the counter, or cover and refrigerate up to 2 hours if you're making them in advance.

While the artichokes are marinating, preheat a gas or charcoal grill to medium-high heat (400°F to 450°F/205°C to 230°C) and lightly oil the grates.

Place the artichokes on the grill and cook for about 15 minutes, flipping occasionally, until charred. Add the lemon halves to the grill and cook to char or until grill marks appear, 2 to 4 minutes.

Serve the artichokes with aioli and lemon halves.

Caribbean Spiced
GRILLED CORN

PREP TIME: 25 minutes   **COOK TIME:** 15 minutes   **YIELD:** Serves 8

Before I developed this recipe, I would have told you that in-season corn is impossible to make more perfect than it already is. But then I started playing around with seasoning blends—specifically one that includes ranch powder (Did she really just do that? Yes, she did.)—and my life has been forever changed. It's an umami bomb in your mouth and would work as a side next to any dish in this book.

TO MAKE THE CARIBBEAN SPICE BLEND: Combine the brown sugar, onion powder, garlic powder, thyme, ground spices, salt, and pepper in a small bowl. Store in an airtight container for up to 6 months.

Preheat a gas or charcoal grill to high heat (450°F to 500°F/230°C to 260°C) and lightly oil the grates.

TO PREPARE THE CORN: While the grill is heating up, melt 3 tablespoons of the butter in a large skillet over medium-high heat. Add the panko and cook, stirring constantly, until the panko is golden brown. Remove from the heat, transfer to a bowl, and let cool for 5 minutes. Sprinkle on the ranch seasoning and cheese and stir well. Set aside until ready to use.

Combine the 1 stick of softened butter and the Caribbean spice blend in a small bowl. Season with salt and pepper.

When the grill is ready, slather the corn with the spiced butter, place on the grill, and cook for 8 to 10 minutes, until charred all over, turning often and basting with the spiced butter.

Remove from the grill and skewer each piece of corn so it has a handle. One at a time, give the corn one more brush of spiced butter. Slather with the mayonnaise and quickly roll into the panko mixture. Repeat until all the corn is covered.

Serve the corn with a squeeze of lime and a sprinkle of Caribbean spice mix.

SPECIAL EQUIPMENT:
8 metal or wooden skewers

FOR THE CARIBBEAN SPICE BLEND:
1 tablespoon light brown sugar
1 tablespoon onion powder
1½ teaspoons garlic powder
1½ teaspoons dried thyme
1½ teaspoons ground ginger
1 teaspoon ground allspice
1 teaspoon ground cinnamon
½ teaspoon ground cloves
½ teaspoon cayenne pepper
1½ teaspoons sea salt
1 teaspoon freshly ground
    black pepper

FOR THE CORN:
3 tablespoons unsalted butter
1 cup (120 g) panko breadcrumbs
2 tablespoons ranch dressing
    seasoning, such as Hidden Valley
¼ cup (25 g) freshly grated
    Parmesan cheese
½ cup (115 g/1 stick) unsalted butter,
    at room temperature
2 tablespoons Caribbean Spice
    Blend (see above), plus more
    for sprinkling
Kosher salt and freshly ground
    black pepper
8 ears corn, shucked
¾ cup (180 ml) mayonnaise
Lime wedges, for serving

Grilled
WEDGE COBB SALAD

PREP TIME: 20 minutes   **COOK TIME:** 20 minutes   **YIELD:** Serves 4

I am not ashamed to admit that I love an old-school wedge salad doused in creamy dressing—but I do think we can give the recipe a little update. First, we're going to grill the romaine lettuce, which can stand up to the heat and take some nice char. Then we're going to whip up an easy buttermilk blue cheese dressing, which is a thousand times better than anything you could get from a bottle. Finally, we're topping it off with the classic bacon crumbles and soft-boiled egg, but also adding avocado for some modern fresh flavor.

FOR THE BLUE CHEESE DRESSING:

¼ cup (60 ml) buttermilk

¼ cup (60 ml) mayonnaise

3 tablespoons sour cream

1 tablespoon red wine vinegar

½ teaspoon garlic powder

1 teaspoon sugar

Kosher salt and freshly ground black pepper

3 ounces (85 g) crumbled blue cheese

A few shakes of vinegar-based hot sauce, such as Tabasco

FOR THE SALAD:

8 slices thick-cut bacon

1 tablespoon distilled white vinegar

2 large eggs, at room temperature

½ baguette, sliced in half widthwise and again lengthwise

2 to 3 tablespoons olive oil

Kosher salt and freshly ground black pepper

2 hearts romaine lettuce, cut in half lengthwise

1 cup (100 g) cherry tomatoes, cut in half

¼ cup (13 g) thinly sliced red onion

3 tablespoons chopped fresh chives

1 avocado, diced

TO MAKE THE BLUE CHEESE DRESSING: Whisk together the buttermilk, mayonnaise, sour cream, vinegar, garlic powder, and sugar in a small bowl. Taste and season with salt (keeping in mind the blue cheese will add saltiness) and pepper, along with a few shakes of hot sauce, then fold in one-half of the blue cheese. Keep covered in the fridge until ready to use.

TO MAKE THE SALAD: Cook the bacon in a large skillet over medium heat for 12 to 15 minutes, until browned and crisp. Remove to a paper towel–lined plate, let cool, and crumble.

Bring a small saucepan filled half-full with water and the vinegar to a boil over medium-high heat. While it's coming up to a boil, fill a bowl with ice water. Lower the eggs into the boiling water and cook for exactly 6 minutes. Remove the eggs from the boiling water and lower them into the ice water to stop the cooking. Let sit for at least 5 minutes, then peel. Hold off on cutting them in half until it's time to dress the salad.

Preheat a gas or charcoal grill to medium-high heat (400°F to 450°F/205°C to 230°C) and lightly oil the grates.

Brush the baguette on all sides with oil and season with salt and pepper. Brush both sides of the lettuce with the oil and season with salt and pepper. Once the grill is hot, place the lettuce and baguette on the grill (baguette cut-side down) and grill for 2 to 3 minutes, until you see some charring. Flip and cook for another 2 to 3 minutes. Remove the lettuce from the heat and place cut-side up on a large platter. Continue grilling the baguette until browned and slightly charred, 3 to 4 more minutes. Remove the baguette from the grill and tear into 1-inch (2.5 cm) pieces.

Cut the soft-boiled eggs in half. Divide the dressing over the grilled romaine and top with the crumbled bacon, tomatoes, sliced onions, the remaining blue cheese, the chives, avocado, eggs, and grilled baguette pieces.

Marinated
GRILLED CABBAGE with Creamy Labneh

PREP TIME: 30 minutes   **MARINATING TIME:** 30 minutes   **COOK TIME:** 16 minutes   **YIELD:** Serves 4

There's this magical thing that happens to cabbage when it's charred. All that bitterness gets tamed by the smoke, and the heat caramelizes its natural sugars. When served over a rich tahini-swirled labneh, it's like tucking into the flossiest bloomin' onion you can imagine.

Preheat a gas or charcoal grill to medium-high heat (400°F to 450°F/205°C to 230°C) and lightly oil the grates.

Whisk together the oil, vinegar, mustard, sumac, oregano, garlic, salt, and pepper in a large bowl. Add the cabbage wedges, toss to coat, and let sit for 30 minutes while the grill heats.

Place the cabbage wedges on the grill, reserving the marinade for serving. Cook for 5 to 8 minutes per side, until lightly charred and tender.

Meanwhile whisk together the labneh, tahini, lemon juice, garlic, 1 tablespoon of the parsley, and 1 tablespoon of the dill in a small bowl.

To serve, place the labneh mixture on a large platter and top with the grilled cabbage. Drizzle with reserved marinade and sprinkle with the remaining 1 tablespoon parsley, remaining 1 tablespoon dill, the pomegranate arils, and toasted pistachios.

½ cup (120 ml) olive oil

¼ cup (60 ml) red wine vinegar

2 teaspoons grainy Dijon mustard

1 teaspoon sumac

1½ teaspoons dried oregano

3 to 4 cloves garlic, minced

½ teaspoon kosher salt

¼ teaspoon freshly ground black pepper

1 large head green cabbage, cored and cut into 8 wedges

1 cup (237 g) labneh

2 tablespoons tahini

2 tablespoons fresh lemon juice

1 clove garlic, grated

2 tablespoons chopped fresh parsley, divided

2 tablespoons chopped fresh dill, divided

¼ cup (45 g) pomegranate arils

¼ cup (30 g) pistachios, toasted and chopped

Balsamic
GRILLED ENDIVE

PREP TIME: 15 minutes **COOK TIME:** 9 minutes **YIELD:** Serves 4

If you've ever had crunchy, bitter raw endive, you'd never, ever imagine that when grilled with a balsamic glaze, it transforms into sticky, sweet, smoky perfection. I like to balance out that sweetness with salty blue cheese and rich walnuts, like a much cooler version of an endive salad.

¼ cup (60 ml) olive oil

2 tablespoons balsamic vinegar

1 teaspoon Dijon mustard

½ teaspoon garlic powder

½ teaspoon onion powder

Kosher salt and freshly ground
   black pepper

6 heads endive, halved lengthwise

¾ cup (160 g) crumbled blue cheese

½ cup (57 g) walnuts, toasted
   and chopped

3 tablespoons chopped fresh chives

Preheat a charcoal or gas grill to medium heat (350°F to 400°F/175°C to 204°C) and lightly oil the grates.

Put the oil, vinegar, mustard, garlic powder, onion powder, ½ teaspoon salt, and ¼ teaspoon pepper in a large bowl and whisk to combine. Add the cut endive to the bowl and gently toss to coat the endive in the marinade.

Once the grill is hot, place the endive on the grill, cut-side down. Cook for 4 to 6 minutes, until nice char marks form. Flip the endive and cook for an additional 2 to 3 minutes. Remove the endive to a serving platter.

Top the grilled endive with the blue cheese, walnuts, chives, and extra black pepper, if desired.

DES

SERTS

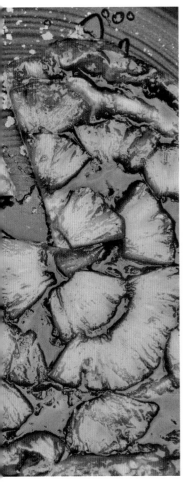

When the weather finally warms up and it's officially grilling season, I do everything in my power to cook outside as much as I can—and that most definitely includes desserts. As I've said before, the grill and the smoker can mimic cooking in the oven, which makes it perfect for baking all the things—cookies, pizookies, cakes, crumbles, galettes. That said, I've also included how you can adapt each of these recipes to make in the oven, which will also deliver perfectly gooey, syrupy, caramelized heaven. No matter how you bake these up, they'll still make ideal pairings for all the savory dishes in this book. So I like to think this chapter is all about taking the party outside—and that's pretty sweet.

One important reminder: All smokers are different in terms of how they maintain heat, so be sure to keep a close eye on your cook times and the visual cues I've given you for when things are done baking!

Honey-Drizzled
GRILLED STONE FRUITS

PREP TIME: 5 minutes **COOK TIME:** 10 minutes **YIELD:** Serves 6 to 8

"Simple" can mean a lot of different things to different people, but we can all agree that grilling your favorite stone fruits—peaches, apricots, plums, nectarines—and topping them with vanilla ice cream and a drizzle of honey is as close as it gets. It's the ultimate easy, breezy summer dessert.

2 ripe peaches

2 ripe nectarines

2 ripe apricots

2 ripe plums

Neutral oil, such as avocado or grapeseed

Vanilla ice cream, for serving

Honey, for finishing

Flaky sea salt, for finishing

Preheat a gas or charcoal grill to medium-high heat (400°F to 450°F/205°C to 230°C) and lightly oil the grates.

Cut the stone fruits in half and remove the pits. Brush the stone fruit halves with a touch of oil. Place on the grill for 2 to 3 minutes, then rotate 90 degrees. The fruit should release from the grill easily before rotating; if it doesn't, continue to grill for another 1 to 2 minutes, until it easily releases. Continue to cook for 2 to 3 minutes more, until grill marks appear and the fruit starts to caramelize.

Remove the fruit from the grill using tongs, place in a bowl, and top with a scoop of ice cream placed in the center of the fruit. Drizzle with honey and finish with a sprinkle of salt.

PRO TIP: Look for freestone or cling-free stone fruit so its easy to twist the stone fruit in half.

S'mores
COOKIES

PREP TIME: 15 minutes   **CHILLING TIME:** 4 to 72 hours   **COOK TIME:** 24 minutes   **YIELD:** Makes 2 dozen

My best friend, Matt, has one major flaw: He hates s'mores. Like, despises them. Instead of ending our relationship over such a monstrous opinion, I made it my mission to change his mind. I took the signature s'mores ingredients and turned them into these chewy, gooey cookies, and lo and behold, success! Great news for Matt because it solved the issue of chocolate and marshmallow seeping out of the sides of a s'more and throwing off the graham-to-goo ratio; great news for me because I can continue being friends with Matt; and great news for you because you have a new fun sweet treat with your favorite summer flavors.

Put the cake flour, bread flour, baking soda, baking powder, and coarse salt in a large bowl and whisk to combine. Set aside.

Combine the butter and sugars in the bowl of an electric mixer and mix on medium-high for about 5 minutes, until fluffy. Add the eggs, one at a time, scraping down the sides of the bowl in between additions. Add the vanilla and mix to combine.

Add the dry ingredients a little at a time and mix until just combined. Add the chocolate chips and fold them into the batter. Cover the dough and refrigerate for at least 4 hours or up to 72 hours.

When ready to bake, preheat the oven to 350°F (175°C). Line two baking sheets with parchment paper.

Scoop up 1 tablespoon of dough, roll it into a ball, and then flatten it. Add a few of the mini marshmallows and 1 or 2 small pieces of graham cracker. Repeat with the remaining dough, marshmallows, and graham cracker pieces.

Place onto the prepared baking sheet, 8 cookies per sheet, and sprinkle the tops with sea salt. Bake the cookies for 10 to 12 minutes, until golden brown. Remove from the oven and transfer the cookies to a cooling rack. If the cookies are a little puffy, bang the pan on the counter to release any excess air pockets. Or use a spatula to flatten the cookies to make them denser.

Store in an airtight container at room temperature, in the fridge or freezer. (I love a freezer cookie!)

2½ cups (240 g) cake flour

2 cups (240 g) bread flour

1¼ teaspoons baking soda

1½ teaspoons baking powder

1½ teaspoons coarse salt

1¼ cups (284 g/2½ sticks) unsalted butter, softened

1¾ cups (340 g) packed dark brown sugar

1 cup (170 g) granulated sugar

2 large eggs

1 tablespoon pure vanilla extract

2 cups (170 g) chocolate chips

Mini marshmallows

2 sleeves graham crackers, broken into ½- to 1-inch (12 mm to 2.5 cm) pieces

Flaky sea salt, for sprinkling

Snickerdoodle
PIZOOKIE

PREP TIME: 15 minutes   **COOK TIME:** 24 minutes   **YIELD:** Serves 6 to 8

I've been a snickerdoodle fan since the good ol' days of carpooling to tennis practice in Tucson, Arizona, when one of the carpool moms would bring them as an after-school treat (looking at you Joann—you're a legend!). I wanted to turn the decadence dial up on these otherwise simple cinnamon-sugar cookies, so I turned them into a "pizza," which guarantees that molten, doughy middle and can be served straight from the skillet with scoops of ice cream on top. I've never looked back.

Nonstick baking spray

1 cup (230 g/2 sticks) unsalted
  butter, at room temperature

1¾ cups (350 g) granulated sugar

2 large eggs

2¾ cups (350 g) all-purpose flour

2 teaspoons cream of tartar

1 tablespoon plus 1½ teaspoons
  ground cinnamon

1 teaspoon baking soda

¼ teaspoon kosher salt

Tillamook Vanilla Bean ice cream,
  for serving

Preheat a pellet smoker (or your oven) to 375°F (190°C), load the hopper with wood pellets, and let it heat up with the lid closed for at least 15 minutes. Spray a 9- to 10-inch (23 to 25 cm) grill-safe (ovenproof) skillet with nonstick baking spray.

Using an electric mixer over medium-high speed, cream together the butter and 1½ cups (300 g) of the sugar for 2 to 3 minutes, until smooth.

Add the eggs, scraping down the sides of the bowl. Add the flour, cream of tartar, 1 tablespoon of the cinnamon, the baking soda, and salt and mix on low speed until everything is incorporated.

To make the topping, combine the remaining ¼ cup (50 g) sugar and remaining 1½ teaspoons cinnamon in a small bowl.

Transfer the batter to the skillet and spread it evenly. Sprinkle the cinnamon sugar on top of the batter. Bake for 22 to 24 minutes, until still slightly gooey in the middle and golden around the edges. Remove from the pellet smoker (or oven) and let rest for a few minutes. Top with scoops of ice cream and serve.

Sheet Pan
COFFEE CRUMB CAKE with Blackberries

PREP TIME: 20 minutes   **COOK TIME:** 25 minutes   **YIELD:** Serves at least 12

One of the things I've loved most about having a toddler sidekick is baking together. This is one recipe Poppy always wants to make with me because she has so much fun sprinkling the lemon–brown sugar crumble over the top, and I'm always happy to oblige because it's the perfect fluffy buttermilk cake studded with jammy blackberries. I tweaked my original recipe a touch by having you bake it in a half sheet pan, which makes it even more grill-friendly and easy to slice and serve.

Preheat a pellet grill (or oven) to 350°F (175°C), load the hopper with wood pellets, and let it heat up with the lid closed for at least 15 minutes. Spray a 17 × 12 × 1-inch (43 × 30.5 × 2.5 cm) half sheet pan with nonstick baking spray.

TO MAKE THE LEMON CRUMB TOPPING: Combine the flour, brown sugar, salt, and lemon zest in a large bowl and pour the melted butter over the mixture. Using your fingers, mix it around until it's crumbly. Set aside.

TO MAKE THE CAKE: Place the blackberries in a medium bowl and toss with 2 tablespoons of the flour. Set aside.

Using an electric mixer, mix the butter and sugar at medium-high speed for 2 to 3 minutes, until pale yellow. Add the lemon zest, whole egg, egg yolk, and vanilla and beat well for an additional 2 to 3 minutes, scraping down the sides, until smooth.

Add the remaining 2 cups (250 g) flour, the baking powder, baking soda, and salt to the mixer and turn it to low speed. Slowly stream in the buttermilk until it is incorporated, scraping down the sides as needed. Fold in the blackberries.

Transfer the batter to the sheet pan. It will create a super thin layer. Top with the crumb topping. Bake for 20 to 25 minutes, until the cake is light and fluffy and baked through. A cake tester inserted into the center of the cake should come out clean. Remove from the pellet grill (or oven) and let cool. Slice directly out of the sheet pan and serve.

FOR THE LEMON CRUMB TOPPING:

1 cup (125 g) all-purpose flour

1 cup (200 g) packed dark brown sugar

1 teaspoon kosher salt

2 tablespoons grated lemon zest

½ cup (115 g/1 stick) unsalted butter, melted

FOR THE CAKE:

Nonstick baking spray

2½ cups (360 g) fresh blackberries

2 cups (250 g) plus 2 tablespoons all-purpose flour

½ cup (115 g/1 stick) unsalted butter, at room temperature

1¼ cups (250 g) granulated sugar

2 tablespoons grated lemon zest

1 large egg

1 large egg yolk

2 teaspoons pure vanilla extract

1 teaspoon baking powder

1 teaspoon baking soda

1 teaspoon kosher salt

1 cup (240 ml) buttermilk

Peach and Blueberry
CRUMBLE

PREP TIME: 20 minutes   **COOK TIME:** 1 hour   **YIELD:** Serves 6

Whether you call it a crumble, a cobbler, or a crisp, it's still going to be a bubbling, gooey, juicy grilled peach and blueberry situation with a ginger and cinnamon-scented oat topping. You could make this on your grill over indirect heat, in your regular oven, or for major wow factor, in a smoker or with a smoker box (applewood is a great pairing). And you can change up the fruit depending on the season or what you find at the market. Any way you slice it, there's a lot to love about this one. And the crème fraîche whipped cream . . . game changer.

FOR THE FILLING:

6 freestone peaches, pitted and cut into 8 pieces each

2 cups (380 g) fresh blueberries

1 tablespoon fresh lemon juice

2 tablespoons spiced rum (optional)

⅓ cup (60 g) packed dark brown sugar

2 tablespoons cornstarch

2 tablespoons unsalted butter, cut into pieces

Pinch of kosher salt

FOR THE CRUMBLE TOPPING:

1 cup (100 g) old-fashioned oats

⅔ cup (120 g) packed dark brown sugar

¾ cup (94 g) all-purpose flour

½ cup (65 g) chopped pecans

½ teaspoon ground cinnamon

½ teaspoon ground ginger

¼ teaspoon freshly grated nutmeg

Pinch of kosher salt

¾ cup (170 g/1½ sticks) unsalted butter, diced

Crème Fraîche Whipped Cream (at right)

Preheat a pellet smoker (or your oven) to 350°F (175°C), load the hopper with wood pellets, and let it heat up with the lid closed for at least 15 minutes. Grease a 9 × 13-inch (29 × 33 cm) baking dish.

TO MAKE THE FILLING: Place all the filling ingredients in a large bowl and mix to combine. Transfer to the prepared baking dish.

TO MAKE THE CRUMBLE TOPPING: Place the oats, brown sugar, flour, pecans, cinnamon, ginger, nutmeg, and salt in a large bowl and stir to combine. Add the butter and, using a pastry cutter, large fork, or your fingers, cut the butter into the oat mixture.

Sprinkle the crisp topping over the fruit, place the baking dish on the pellet grill, and close the lid. Bake for 50 to 60 minutes, until the crumble is browned and the filling is bubbling. Remove from the smoker and let cool slightly. Serve with crème fraîche whipped cream or ice cream.

CRÈME FRAÎCHE WHIPPED CREAM
YIELD: Makes 2 cups (480 ml)

⅓ cup (80 g) crème fraîche

¼ cup (31 g) powdered sugar

½ teaspoon pure vanilla extract

1¼ cups (300 ml) heavy cream

Chill the bowl and whisk of your stand mixer in the freezer for 5 to 10 minutes while you gather the ingredients. This ensures maximum volume of the whipped cream.

Place all the ingredients into the chilled bowl and whisk, starting on low speed and slowly increasing the speed to medium-high, until soft peaks are formed. Remove to a bowl, cover with plastic wrap, and refrigerate until ready to serve, or up to 2 to 3 days if you're prepping ahead.

Brown Butter
ALMOND CAKE with Poached Strawberries

PREP TIME: 20 minutes   **COOK TIME:** 55 minutes   **YIELD:** Serves 8

I'm all about solid, versatile recipes that you can keep in your back pocket and dress up with all sorts of different flavors depending on your mood and what's in season. In this case, we're taking a rich, dense brown butter cake and giving it the royal treatment by infusing it with cherrywood on the smoker, then drizzling it with rosé-poached strawberries.

Preheat a pellet smoker (or your oven) to 325°F (163°C), load the hopper with wood pellets (any wood will do here, but cherrywood is best), and let it heat up with the lid closed for at least 15 minutes. Grease a 9 × 9-inch (23 × 23 cm) baking pan on the bottom and sides of the pan with butter, line the bottom with parchment paper, and grease again.

TO MAKE THE CAKE: Whisk together the all-purpose flour, almond flour, baking powder, and salt in a medium bowl. Set aside.

Put the butter in a medium stainless-steel skillet (or other light-colored skillet) over medium heat. Once melted, the butter will begin to foam and sizzle. Keep stirring or swirling the pan for 3 to 5 minutes, until the butter turns golden brown, the foam subsides slightly, and the milk solids on the bottom get toasted. Remove from the heat to a large heatproof bowl.

Whisk the sugar into the melted butter until incorporated. Allow to cool for 5 minutes. Whisk in the eggs, one at a time. Add the lemon zest, vanilla, and almond extract. Stir to combine. Slowly add the dry ingredients to the butter mixture and mix until incorporated. Pour the batter into the prepared pan and smooth out the top. Sprinkle the sliced almonds and coarse sugar over the cake.

Place the cake on the pellet smoker and bake for 35 to 40 minutes, until a toothpick inserted into the center of the pan comes out clean. Remove the cake from the smoker, place on a wire rack, and let cool completely in the pan, 1 to 2 hours. The cake can be made the day before and kept covered with plastic wrap on the counter.

TO MAKE THE ROSÉ-POACHED STRAWBERRIES: While the cake is cooling, in a medium saucepan, combine the wine, honey, and lemon zest and bring to a boil over medium-high heat. Reduce the heat to medium and cook until reduced to about 1 cup (240 ml), 12 to 15 minutes. Add the vanilla bean paste, strawberries, and salt and cook for 2 minutes more, until well combined. Remove to a heatproof bowl and let cool to room temperature.

TO FINISH: Whisk together the labneh, honey, and vanilla bean paste in a small bowl. To serve, slice the cake however you like and top with the labneh and poached strawberries.

FOR THE CAKE:
1¼ cups (156 g) all-purpose flour
½ cup (96 g) almond flour
½ teaspoon baking powder
½ teaspoon kosher salt
¾ cup (170 g/1½ sticks) unsalted butter, plus more for greasing the pan
1¼ cups (250 g) granulated sugar
2 large eggs
1 teaspoon grated lemon zest
1 teaspoon pure vanilla extract
1 teaspoon almond extract
½ cup (46 g) sliced almonds
1 tablespoon coarse sanding sugar

FOR THE ROSÉ-POACHED STRAWBERRIES:
2 cups (480 ml) rosé wine
2 tablespoons honey
1 (3-inch/7.5 cm) strip lemon zest
1 teaspoon vanilla bean paste
1 pound (455 g) fresh strawberries, hulled and halved
Pinch of kosher salt

FOR THE LABNEH:
2 cups (474 g) labneh
1 tablespoon honey
1 teaspoon vanilla bean paste

pineapple
TARTE TATIN

PREP TIME: 30 minutes   **COOK TIME:** 1 hour 15 minutes   **YIELD:** Serves 6

All I can say about this creation from Adam's genius mind is that it's a classic French tarte Tatin meets old-school pineapple upside-down cake. It's sweet and syrupy with a little bad-girl edge from the smoke. And because we're all about keeping things simple here, the recipe calls for store-bought puff pastry instead of having to make your own dough.

1 sheet store-bought puff pastry, thawed

1 medium pineapple

¼ cup (57 g/½ stick) unsalted butter, at room temperature

¾ cup (150 g) granulated sugar

1 tablespoon corn syrup

¼ teaspoon ground cinnamon (optional)

⅛ teaspoon freshly grated nutmeg (optional)

½ teaspoon fine sea salt

Ice cream, crème fraîche, or whipped cream, for serving

Line a baking sheet with parchment paper. On a lightly floured surface, roll the puff pastry into a 12- to 13-inch (30 to 33 cm) square. Place on the prepared baking sheet and poke it with a fork all over. Place in the refrigerator until ready to use.

Remove the top, bottom, and skin from the pineapple. Slice in half from top to bottom. Carefully remove the firm core from each half with a paring knife and cut each half into ½-inch (1.25 cm) half-moons. Lay the sliced pineapple on a baking sheet lined with paper towels, top with more paper towels, and press down to blot out extra moisture. Let sit for 10 to 15 minutes.

Preheat a pellet smoker (or your oven) to 375°F (190°C), load the hopper with wood pellets, and let it heat up with the lid closed for at least 15 minutes. Slather the bottom of a 10-inch (25 cm) cast-iron skillet with the softened butter, sprinkle on the sugar, then add the corn syrup, cinnamon and nutmeg, if desired, and salt. Place on the grill of the smoker, close the lid, and cook for 5 minutes.

Open the lid and check the sugar; give it a stir, close the lid, and cook for another 5 minutes. Continue stirring every 5 minutes and then closing the lid for about 20 minutes total to develop a rich caramel. Take care not to let it burn. Starting in the center of the pan, carefully arrange the pineapple slices around the pan, slightly overlapping. You'll have some pineapple slices left over. You can tear them into pieces to fit if needed.

Remove the puff pastry from the refrigerator and carefully place it on top of the pineapple, tucking the edges in slightly. This won't be perfect—it'll be rustic!

Close the lid of the smoker and cook for 35 to 55 minutes, until the puff pastry is golden brown. (It will take about 40 minutes in the oven.) You can check a few times, but remember that every time you open the lid the temp will drop slightly, potentially extending the cooking time.

Remove the pan from the smoker, let cool for 5 minutes, then carefully turn the tarte Tatin out onto a large plate. Serve hot or warm with ice cream, crème fraîche, or whipped cream.

Grilled
FIGS with Brown Sugar Balsamic No-Churn Ice Cream

PREP TIME: 20 minutes   **FREEZING TIME:** 4 to 24 hours   **COOK TIME:** 10 minutes   **YIELD:** Serves 6 (with leftover ice cream)

Raise your hand if you've invested in an ice cream machine and can count on that one hand how many times you've used it. I'm guessing it's quite a few of us. I get it; we all want to make our own custom ice cream anytime the mood strikes. But it turns out that you don't need a fancy gadget or prechilled mixing bowls to do it. This lusciously creamy ice cream comes together in no time, but you'd never guess it was based on the sophisticated sweet-tart balsamic ripple. Top it with your favorite fruit and call it a day!

Combine the vinegar and brown sugar in a small saucepan and heat over medium heat, stirring frequently, until it comes to a simmer and the sugar dissolves. Turn the heat down to low and continue to cook for 7 to 10 minutes, stirring occasionally, until the mixture reduces to about 2 tablespoons. Set the balsamic glaze aside to cool completely.

Put the sweetened condensed milk and vanilla in a large bowl and whisk to combine. Set aside.

Pour the cream into a separate large bowl. Using an electric hand mixer, beat the cream until stiff peaks form, about 5 minutes. Add the whipped cream to the sweetened condensed milk in three increments, folding in each batch of cream before adding the next. Transfer half of the mixture to a 9 × 5-inch (29 × 13 cm) loaf pan. Drizzle half of the balsamic glaze on top and use a butter knife to swirl it into the ice cream base. Pour the remaining ice cream base on top. Top with the remaining glaze and swirl once again into the ice cream base. Cover loosely with plastic wrap and transfer to the freezer to set for at least 4 hours or up to 24 hours.

Once the ice cream has set, grill the figs. Preheat a gas or charcoal grill to medium heat (350°F to 450°F/175°C to 230°C). If you would like to do this without a grill, use a grill pan on your indoor stove.

Cut the figs in half lengthwise and place them in a medium bowl. Drizzle with the oil and toss to coat. Transfer the figs to the grill, cut-side down. Grill for about 2 minutes, or until nice char marks form. Flip the figs and cook for an additional 2 to 3 minutes, until softened. Transfer to a plate. To serve, scoop the ice cream into bowls and top with the grilled figs.

¼ cup (60 ml) balsamic vinegar

2 tablespoons light brown sugar

1 (14-ounce/397 g) can sweetened condensed milk

1 teaspoon pure vanilla extract

2 cups (480 ml) heavy cream

6 fresh figs

1 tablespoon olive oil

Raspberry GALETTE with Whipped Cream

PREP TIME: 20 minutes   **CHILLING TIME:** 1 hour 20 minutes   **COOK TIME:** 50 minutes   **YIELD:** Serves 6

Hot take, but I've never been a huge fan of pie. Maybe it's the fuss of all the crimping; maybe it's the imbalanced ratio of too much filling to too little crust, but I've joined Team Galette and my allegiance has never wavered. Galettes, or rustic, free-form pies, are much more my speed with their flaky, buttery crusts and just the right amount of cooked-fruit filling. I love making this with raspberries for that gorgeous magenta pop of color.

1¼ cups (156 g) all-purpose flour, plus more for dusting

½ cup (115 g/1 stick) unsalted butter, cut into small pieces (pea- to walnut-size)

¼ teaspoon kosher salt

3 to 4 tablespoons ice water

3 cups (369 g) fresh raspberries

1½ teaspoons grated orange zest

¼ cup (50 g) granulated sugar

2 teaspoons cornstarch

¼ teaspoon kosher salt

1 large egg

1 tablespoon raw sugar

1 cup (240 ml) heavy cream

2 tablespoons powdered sugar

½ teaspoon vanilla bean paste

Combine the flour, butter, and salt in a large bowl; with clean hands, mix together until it looks like coarse meal with some lumps in it. Sprinkle ice water over the mixture and stir lightly with a fork. Squeeze a handful of dough together. If it doesn't keep together, add a bit more water. Once it comes together nicely, form the dough into a disk 5 inches (12.5 cm) across. Wrap the disk in plastic wrap and chill for about 1 hour.

In the meantime, preheat a pellet smoker (or your oven) to 375°F (190°C), load the hopper with wood pellets, and let it heat up with the lid closed for at least 15 minutes. Line a sheet pan with parchment paper.

Put the raspberries, ½ teaspoon of the orange zest, the granulated sugar, cornstarch, and salt in a large bowl and toss to combine. Set aside.

Place the chilled pie dough on a well-floured work surface. Sprinkle some flour on top of the disk. Thump each side of the disk with your rolling pin several times. Sprinkle more flour on top if needed to keep the pin from sticking and roll the dough out from the center in all directions into a 13-inch (33 cm) round. Transfer the dough to the prepared baking sheet.

Add the berries to the center of the dough, leaving a 2-inch (5 cm) border all around. Fold the dough around the filling, pleating as necessary.

Whisk the egg with 1 tablespoon cold water. Use a pastry brush to brush the egg wash on the exposed crust. Sprinkle the raw sugar over the crust and put in the freezer for 20 minutes to chill.

Transfer the galette to the pellet smoker and bake for 45 to 50 minutes, until the crust is golden brown and the center is bubbling.

While the galette is baking, combine the heavy cream, powdered sugar, vanilla bean paste, and remaining 1 teaspoon orange zest in an electric mixer and beat until just combined and creamy; avoid overwhipping. Cover and refrigerate until ready to use.

Remove the galette from the pellet smoker and let sit for 10 minutes. Slice, top with whipped cream, and serve.

Dinner Party

STEAK POTATOES

This retro spread is giving three-martini steakhouse lunch vibes with all the 1960s glam. It's a little cheeky, a little over the top, and just the right amount of delicious.

Grilled Tomahawk Steak

Baked Potatoes with Garlic Butter

Grilled Caesar Salad with Garlic Croutons

Make-Ahead Martini with Blue Cheese–Stuffed Olives

Chocolate and Strawberry Baked Alaska

Grilled
TOMAHAWK STEAK

PREP TIME: 5 minutes   **RESTING TIME:** 1 hour 10 minutes   **COOK TIME:** 55 minutes   **YIELD:** Serves 4

An hour before cooking, remove the steak from the refrigerator to bring it to room temperature. About 30 minutes before cooking, season it generously with salt and pepper. A good rule of thumb is to use about 1 teaspoon of salt per pound of meat and a third of that amount of pepper.

Set up the grill for indirect cooking by preheating one half of the grill to medium-low heat (225°F/110°C is perfect) and lightly oil the grates. If using charcoal, set up the briquettes underneath half of the grill grate.

Transfer the steak to the indirect side of the grill and cook for 45 minutes, or until an instant-read thermometer registers 115°F (46°C) in the middle part of the meat.

Remove the steak from the grill, increase the heat to high heat (450°F to 500°F/232°C to 260°C), and grill both sides for 3 to 5 minutes per side, until nice grill marks have formed and until your desired doneness. Use grill tongs to stand the steak up and sear all the edges, forming a nice crust around the entire steak. My preference is an internal temperature of 140°F (60°C).

Remove the steak from the grill and let it rest for 10 minutes. To serve, use a sharp knife to cut along the bone removing the meat. Slice and serve. Season with extra salt and pepper if desired. Garnish with a sprinkling of chopped herbs.

1 tomahawk rib-eye steak, 2 inches (5 cm) thick, with rib bone still attached

Kosher salt, plus more for serving

Freshly ground black pepper, plus more for serving

Chopped herbs, such as rosemary and thyme, for garnish

Baked POTATOES

with Garlic Butter

PREP TIME: 20 minutes   **COOK TIME:** 1 hour 15 minutes   **YIELD:** Serves 4 to 8

---

1 whole bulb garlic

Olive oil

Kosher salt and freshly ground
    black pepper

4 large russet potatoes

½ cup (115 g/1 stick) unsalted butter,
    at room temperature

Sour cream, for serving

Chopped fresh chives, for serving

Preheat a gas or charcoal grill to medium-high heat (400°F to 450°F/205°C to 230°C).

Cut the top quarter off the garlic, exposing the cloves. Place the garlic on a 6 × 6-inch (15 × 15 cm) piece of aluminum foil. Add 2 teaspoons oil and season with a pinch each of salt and pepper. Wrap the foil around the garlic, completely enclosing it. Set aside.

Use a fork to poke each potato 5 times. Place the potatoes and 3 tablespoons oil in a bowl and add 2 teaspoons salt. Mix to coat the potatoes in the oil and salt. Place each potato in a 12 × 12-inch (30 × 30 cm) piece of foil. Pour any remaining oil and salt in the bowl over the potatoes. Wrap the foil around each potato, completely enclosing them.

Transfer the potatoes and garlic bulb to the grill. Cook for 35 to 45 minutes, until the garlic is tender. Remove from the grill and let cool. Continue cooking the potatoes an additional 20 to 30 minutes, turning occasionally, until easily pierced with a fork.

Once the garlic has cooled slightly, carefully remove the cloves from the papery skin and place in a small bowl. Mash the garlic with a fork, add the butter, and mix until thoroughly combined. Add ¼ teaspoon salt and a pinch of pepper and stir to combine. Refrigerate until the potatoes are cooked.

When the potatoes are tender, remove them from the grill and allow them to cool for 5 minutes. Unwrap the potatoes. Cut them in half and slather them with the garlic butter, sour cream, and chives. Serve immediately.

Grilled
CAESAR SALAD

with Garlic Croutons

PREP TIME: 5 minutes **RESTING TIME:** 1 hour **COOK TIME:** 35 minutes **YIELD:** Serves 4

Preheat a charcoal or gas grill to medium heat (350°F to 400°F/175°C to 204°C) and lightly oil the grates.

TO MAKE THE DRESSING: Put all the ingredients in a wide-mouth jar and blend with an immersion blender until evenly combined and smooth. Taste and season with more salt and pepper as needed. Set aside until ready to serve.

TO MAKE THE CROUTONS: Heat the oil in a medium nonstick skillet. Add the torn bread and cook, stirring often, until light golden brown. Add the butter and garlic and stir continuously for 30 seconds to 1 minute, until the garlic is fragrant and golden. Season with salt and pepper. Transfer the croutons to a plate to cool.

TO GRILL THE ROMAINE HEARTS: Use a pastry brush to lightly brush the cut sides of the romaine hearts with oil. Transfer to the grill, cut-side down. Grill for 3 to 5 minutes, until char marks form. Transfer the lettuce to a serving platter, cut-side up. Drizzle with the dressing and top with the croutons and cheese. Season with salt and pepper, if desired.

FOR THE DRESSING:
¼ cup (60 ml) mayonnaise

2 teaspoons Dijon mustard

2 teaspoons anchovy paste

1 teaspoon Worcestershire sauce

¼ cup (60 ml) fresh lemon juice

2 cloves garlic, smashed

½ cup (120 ml) olive oil

⅓ cup (35 g) grated Parmesan cheese

Kosher salt and freshly ground black pepper to taste

FOR THE CROUTONS:
2 tablespoons olive oil

2 slices French bread, torn into small pieces (about 1½ cups/70 g)

1 tablespoon unsalted butter

2 cloves garlic, minced

Kosher salt and freshly ground black pepper

FOR THE SALAD:
4 romaine hearts, root trimmed, halved

Olive oil

½ cup (50 g) shaved Parmesan cheese

Kosher salt and freshly ground black pepper (optional)

Make-Ahead MARTINI

with Blue Cheese–Stuffed Olives

PREP TIME: 30 minutes   **FREEZING TIME:** 6 hours   **YIELD:** Serves 4 to 8

FOR THE MAKE-AHEAD MARTINI:

1 (750 ml) bottle vodka

3 ounces (90 ml) dry vermouth

2 ounces (60 ml) water

3 ounces (90 ml) Castelvetrano olive brine

FOR THE BLUE CHEESE–STUFFED OLIVES:

4 ounces (113 g) Roquefort cheese

2 ounces (57 g) cream cheese

1 tablespoon heavy cream

¼ teaspoon freshly ground black pepper

20 pitted Castelvetrano olives

TO MAKE THE MARTINI: Remove 1 cup (240 ml) vodka from the bottle and save for another use. Add the vermouth, water, and olive brine. Put the lid on and shake to combine. Freeze for at least 6 hours before serving.

TO MAKE THE STUFFED OLIVES: Combine the blue cheese, cream cheese, cream, and pepper in a food processor and process until smooth. Transfer the cheese mixture to a zip-top bag or piping bag. Snip off the tip of the bag and gently pipe the mixture into each of the olives. Store in an airtight container in the fridge until ready to use.

Serve the cocktails in martini glasses garnished with 3 to 4 olives skewered on a cocktail pick.

Chocolate and Strawberry
BAKED ALASKA

PREP TIME: 40 minutes   **COOK TIME:** 45 minutes   **FREEZING TIME:** 4 hours   **YIELD:** Serves 6

Preheat the oven to 325°F (163°C). Spray a 9 × 9-inch (23 × 23 cm) baking pan with nonstick baking spray and line with parchment paper. Spray again and set aside.

Combine the chocolate and butter in a small saucepan. Place over medium-low heat and stir until smooth. Add 1¼ cups (250 g) of the sugar and stir to combine. Remove from the heat for 15 minutes to cool slightly. Add the eggs and vanilla and whisk to combine. Add the flour and salt and mix until just incorporated. Pour the mixture into the prepared pan and pop in the oven for 30 to 35 minutes, until set.

Remove from the oven to a wire rack and let cool for 1 hour. Remove from the pan and cut in half. You should have two pieces about 9 x 4½ inches (23 × 11.5 cm). Refrigerate until ready to use. Don't assemble until the brownies are completely cool. If you want to rush this step, you can freeze the brownies.

Spray a 9 × 5 × 3-inch (23 × 13 × 7.5 cm) loaf pan with baking spray and line with plastic wrap, leaving a 3-inch (7.5 cm) overhang on both sides. Remove the brownie layers from the refrigerator and spread ¼ cup (80 g) strawberry preserves onto the top of each layer and set aside.

Spread half of the strawberry ice cream into the loaf pan, making sure to get it into all the corners. Place one of the brownie layers into the pan, strawberry preserves–side down, and firmly press the layer into place. Repeat with the remaining ice cream and brownie layer. Fold over the plastic wrap and place in the freezer for at least 4 hours or, best, overnight.

To make the meringue topping, place the egg whites in the bowl (make sure it's very clean) of a stand mixer fitted with the whisk attachment. Beat on medium-low speed until foamy with soft peaks. Stop the mixer and make the sugar syrup.

Nonstick baking spray

¾ cup (170 g) dark chocolate chips

½ cup (115 g/1 stick) unsalted butter

2¼ cups (450 g) granulated sugar, divided

3 large eggs, at room temperature

2 teaspoons pure vanilla extract

⅓ cup (40 g) all-purpose flour

Pinch of kosher salt

½ cup (160 g) strawberry preserves

1 quart (960 ml) strawberry ice cream, softened

4 large egg whites, at room temperature

⅓ cup (70 ml) water

Fresh strawberries, for garnish

(recipe continues)

Combine the remaining 1 cup (200 g) sugar and the water in a small sauce-pan and bring to a boil over medium-high heat. Cook until it reaches a temperature of 250°F (120°C) on a candy thermometer. Remove from the heat.

Turn the stand mixer back on and slowly work the speed back to medium. Slowly drizzle the sugar syrup into the egg whites down the side of the bowl, avoiding the whisk. Continue beating until stiff and glossy, about 5 minutes. The bowl of the mixer will still be slightly warm.

Remove the loaf pan from the freezer and unmold onto a serving platter. Using an offset spatula, spread the meringue all over the top and sides, swirling and creating peaks. Place back into the freezer for at least 20 minutes, until frozen solid or you're ready to serve. (This can keep in the freezer for up to 5 days; cover with plastic once the meringue is frozen solid.)

Torch the meringue right before serving. (You can also brown the meringue by placing it in a preheated 450°F/230°C oven or the broiler for 3 to 4 minutes.) Slice and serve with fresh strawberries.

DRINKS

Passing the reins to one of my very best friends to introduce this chapter . . .

"Hello! I'm Zack, one of Gaby's best friends and her cocktail consigliere. Once upon a time at SXSW in Austin, Gaby and I were sitting at a bar on Congress trying every cocktail and bar snack on the menu. I'm pretty sure I spent my entire per diem on that happy hour, but it was a great talk that I still think about years later. We covered all our big plans for the future, from her burgeoning career as a chef, to my plan to marry her childhood best friend. Since then, I did in fact marry her best friend (nice!) and had the honor of officiating Gaby and Thomas's wedding. How is that relevant to this book? Well, I think it's fair to say that Gaby trusts me. And that goes double for my cocktail recipes. This chapter is dedicated to the years I've spent trying to re-create my favorite cocktails at home. From my summer go-to, the Gold Rush, to our riff on a Broken Negroni, we still enjoy sharing these libations together . . . only now we do it while we watch our wild animals (children) run around on warm California afternoons. Here's to you joining us on the adventure—cheers!"

Hugo SPRITZ

YIELD: Makes 2 drinks

We all know and love an Aperol spritz, the popular Italian cocktail that consists of the orange-flavored aperitif plus prosecco with a splash of sparkling water. But I think it's time for the Hugo spritz to have its moment. This softer, more floral cocktail originated in northern Italy and uses elderflower liqueur instead of Aperol. Whether you enjoy one as a refreshing pre-meal beverage or offer it to guests alongside some grilled artichokes (see page 158), it's giving major dolce vita summer vibes and I'm here for it.

1 ounce (30 ml) St-Germain

A few fresh mint leaves, plus more for garnish

Ice

8 ounces (240 ml) prosecco, chilled

4 ounces (120 ml) sparkling water, chilled

Combine the St-Germain and mint in a cocktail shaker. Gently muddle and let sit for 3 minutes. Add ice and shake. Transfer to 2 glasses and add half of the prosecco and sparkling water to each. Stir briefly and gently to combine. Garnish with mint and serve.

Summer
SANGRIA

YIELD: Serves 6 to 8

There's a reason sangria has been an entertaining staple since pretty much forever—everyone loves it, it can be prepped a day or two in advance, and it is endlessly customizable to the season or meal. This version is peak summer vibes with its sliced strawberries and peaches, basil and mint, and blend of white and pink wine. If you come to my house anytime between June and September, there's a really good chance a pitcher of this will be on the table.

Combine the sugar and brandy in a large pitcher and stir until the sugar dissolves. Add the strawberries, peaches, and wines and stir again. Add the basil. Refrigerate the sangria for at least 6 hours before serving.

To serve, fill a glass with ice and pour in enough sangria to fill three-fourths of the glass. Finish with a splash of club soda and garnish with basil and mint.

⅓ cup (60 g) granulated sugar

⅓ cup (70 ml) brandy

2 cups (332 g) sliced fresh strawberries

1 cup (168 g) sliced fresh peaches

1 (750 ml) bottle rosé wine

1 (750 ml) bottle Sauvignon Blanc wine

½ cup (20 g) fresh basil leaves, plus more for garnish

Ice

1 cup (240 ml) chilled club soda or sparkling water

Fresh mint leaves, for garnish

Broken
NEGRONI

YIELD: Makes 1 drink

For this classic cocktail, we're going back to Italy but by way of California. Zack's spin on the traditional recipe adds a splash of prosecco, which balances out the bitterness of the Campari without messing with the citrus flavors. I highly recommend using prosecco from a can, so you don't end up wasting the rest of your bottle of prosecco. But that may not be an issue for some of us—zero judgment here!

Ice

1½ ounces (45 ml) Campari

1 (8.5-ounce/250 ml) can Casa Luigi Secco Bianco Prosecco (or other brand of choice)

1½ ounces (45 ml) sweet vermouth

3 dashes orange bitters

Orange twist or dehydrated orange slice, for garnish

Fill a rocks glass with ice and add the Campari, prosecco, vermouth, and bitters. Stir well to chill, decorate with your choice of orange garnish, and serve immediately.

Strawberry
DAIQUIRI

YIELD: Makes 4 drinks

Daiquiris haven't always been considered the classy girl's cocktail, but I assure you that when you make them with fresh in-season strawberries, they get an instant glow-up. Just promise me you'll wait for those good berries! They make all the difference in getting that perfectly sweet note of summer strawberry flavor.

Put the strawberries in a freezer container and freeze for at least 4 hours.

Make a simple syrup by combining the sugar with ¼ cup (60 ml) water in a small saucepan. Bring to a boil over medium-high heat, then lower the heat and simmer 2 to 3 minutes to dissolve the sugar. Remove from the heat and cool to room temperature.

Place the frozen strawberries, ¼ cup (60 ml) simple syrup, the lime juice, rum, and ice cubes in a blender and blend until smooth. Divide into 4 glasses and serve with an additional strawberry garnish.

Store remaining simple syrup in the fridge to use in future batches.

1 pound (455 g) fresh strawberries, plus 4 strawberries for garnish
¼ cup (60 ml) sugar
¼ cup (60 ml) fresh lime juice
1 cup (240 ml) light rum
1 cup (240 g) ice cubes

Grilled Lime
MOJITO

YIELD: Makes 2 drinks

You know those drinks that transport you back to your favorite vacation spot with the first sip? That's a mojito for me! The combination of rum, lime, and mint in this Cuban punch is pretty much impossible to improve upon, so I'm not going to mess too much with a good thing. But I did discover that by tossing the limes on the grill before juicing them they take on a deeper, sweeter flavor with just a hint of smoke. And trust me, no one's going to be mad about that.

1 medium lime, cut in half

¼ cup (7 g) fresh mint leaves

3 tablespoons granulated sugar, or to taste

Ice cubes

3 ounces (90 ml) white rum

1 cup (240 ml) club soda

Place the lime halves on a grill (you can throw in with whatever else you're making and it will be fine) and grill for 2 to 3 minutes, until you get char marks and the juices start getting juicy.

Divide the mint leaves between 2 glasses. Squeeze the juice from the lime into the glasses. Use a muddler to crush and release the mint oils and lime juice in the glasses. Divide the sugar between the glasses and muddle again to combine. Do not strain.

Fill the glass almost to the top with ice. Pour in the rum and fill the glasses with club soda and serve.

Pineapple
SMASH

YIELD: Makes 2 drinks

A smash is basically any spirit mixed with fresh fruit juice and some sparkling water or club soda to give it a little fizz. It's the perfect equation for an endless number of tasty variations, and this one happens to be one of my favorites. Pineapple and lime will always be a winning combo, plus some tequila (or gin or rum), and it'll hands-down be your new grilling out summer cocktail.

Muddle the mint and lime juice in the bottom of a cocktail shaker. Add the tequila and pineapple juice along with a few pieces of ice and secure the lid onto the shaker. Shake for 30 seconds, or until the liquid is chilled.

Pour the cocktail, muddled bits and all, into 2 ice-filled cocktail glasses and top with a spritz of club soda. Serve immediately.

1 or 2 sprigs mint

1 ounce (30 ml) fresh lime juice

4 ounces (120 ml) blanco tequila, gin, or clear rum

6 ounces (180 ml) pineapple juice

Ice

Club soda

Pink G+T

YIELD: Makes 2 drinks

When Thomas and I were on safari in South Africa, one of our favorite new traditions that we brought home with us was the "sundowner," or having a happy hour cocktail at sunset. The drink that was usually on offer was the very traditional gin and tonic, but I of course wanted to come up with my own spin for our sundowners at home. A splash of Lillet Rosé and grapefruit-infused liqueur makes this cocktail not only adorably rosy, but also refreshingly light and easy to drink.

---

3 ounces (90 ml) gin

1½ ounces (45 ml) Lillet Rosé

1 ounce (30 ml) pamplemousse rose liqueur

½ ounce (15 ml) Aperol

Ice

Tonic water

2 grapefruit twists

Combine the gin, Lillet Rosé, pamplemousse rose liqueur, and Aperol in a cocktail shaker and stir.

Pour equal amounts into 2 collins glasses filled with ice. Top with tonic water and grapefruit twists to garnish.

GOLD RUSH on Ice

YIELD: Makes 2 drinks

It took me a long time to get on the bourbon train, but here we are! This cocktail was the perfect introduction because the naturally sweet Meyer lemon juice both brightens and balances, and I also love that it's served over crushed ice rather than a big rock. Give me a grown-up slushie moment any day of the week.

Combine 1 cup (240 ml) water and the honey in a small saucepan. Bring to a slow boil over medium heat until the honey is dissolved. Remove from the heat and let cool before transferring to an airtight container. Store in the fridge and use as needed.

Combine the bourbon, lemon juice, and 1½ ounces (45 ml) honey simple syrup in a cocktail shaker with crushed ice and shake until well chilled.

Strain into 2 glasses over crushed ice and garnish each glass with a lemon twist.

1 cup (240 ml) honey
4 ounces (120 ml) bourbon
1½ ounces (45 ml) fresh Meyer lemon juice
Crushed ice
2 lemon twists, for garnish

Big-Batch
CITRUS PUNCH

YIELD: Makes about 7 cups (if using rum)

If I could teach you just one thing to make entertaining easier, let it be to batch prep the cocktails in advance. That way, when guests arrive, you only need to point them in the direction of your expertly assembled pitcher instead of running around taking drink orders. Less work for you, more delicious beverages for your guests—everybody wins. I particularly love this recipe because it's a fresh, fruity punch that makes it feel like you should be on vacation. And honestly, when paired with any of the recipes from this book, it's as close as you can get in your own backyard.

---

2 cups (480 ml) pineapple juice

2 cups (480 ml) tangerine or orange juice

¼ cup (60 ml) fresh lime juice

¼ cup (60 ml) fresh lemon juice

⅓ cup (70 ml) grenadine

2 cups (480 ml) light rum or coconut rum (optional)

Ice

Lime or orange slices, for garnish

Maraschino cherries, for garnish

Pour the pineapple juice, tangerine juice, lime juice, lemon juice, grenadine, and rum (if using) into a large pitcher and stir to combine. Chill in the refrigerator until ready to serve.

Serve the punch over ice and garnish with lime or orange slices and maraschino cherries.

ODDS

+ ENDS

+ Other Random Things for Peak Grilling Vibes

Let's be clear about one thing: The recipes in this book are perfect. Full stop. End of story. That said, in my opinion, there is always room for that extra little something to really make a dish special. So while you can't go wrong picking a dish and running with it, these sauces, seasonings, condiments, and other accompaniments add just that much more dimension and flavor. I also love having these recipes handy for nights when I want to grill but want to mix and match with whatever I have in my fridge or freezer. That's when I reach for one of these all-purpose rubs or marinades. Maybe finish things off with some caramelized onions or a slather of compound butter (or both!). Or whip up a batch of no-frills burgers and offer up your very own "secret" burger sauce or homemade ketchup—does it get more impressive than that? These are your secret weapons for taking super-basic, super-simple recipes and transforming them into the most delicious versions of themselves.

HOMEMADE PICKLES (AND OTHER VEGETABLES)

PREP TIME: 10 minutes
MARINATING TIME: 24 hours
COOK TIME: 10 minutes
YIELD: Makes 1 quart (940 ml)

1¼ cups (300 ml) water
¾ cup (180 ml) rice vinegar
1 teaspoon kosher salt
1 teaspoon sugar
2 teaspoons pickling spice
½ teaspoon red pepper flakes

1 pound (455 g) Persian cucumbers, sliced into coins or spears (you could also use this for carrots + jalapeños + green beans + cauliflower)
6 large sprigs dill
3 cloves garlic, smashed and peeled

Combine the water, vinegar, salt, sugar, pickling spice, and pepper flakes in a small saucepan. Bring to a simmer over medium heat.

Meanwhile, combine the cucumbers, dill, and garlic in a heat-resistant quart-size jar and set aside.

Once the vinegar mixture comes to a simmer, turn off the heat. Pour the mixture over the cucumbers and let cool to room temperature. Cover the jar and store in the refrigerator for at least 24 hours before enjoying.

PICKLED RED ONIONS

PREP TIME: 5 minutes
MARINATING TIME: 1 hour
YIELD: Makes about 1½ cups (360 ml)

1 cup (240 ml) apple cider vinegar
1 tablespoon sugar

1½ teaspoons kosher salt
1 medium red onion, thinly sliced

Whisk the vinegar, sugar, salt, and 1 cup (240 ml) water in a small bowl until the sugar and salt dissolve. Place the onion in a 1-pint (480 ml) jar and pour the vinegar mixture over it. Let sit at room temperature for 1 hour before using. Store in the fridge for 1 to 2 months and use as needed.

CARAMELIZED ONIONS

PREP TIME: 5 minutes
COOK TIME: 35 minutes
YIELD: Makes about 1 cup (225 g)

2 tablespoons unsalted butter
3 tablespoons olive oil, divided
2 large yellow onions (about 1 pound/455 g), peeled and sliced ¼ inch (6 mm) thick

Kosher salt and freshly cracked black pepper
1 teaspoon fresh thyme leaves

Melt the butter in 1 tablespoon of the oil in a large saucepan over medium-high heat. Add the onions and season with salt and pepper.

Cook, stirring occasionally, for 15 minutes. Reduce the heat to medium and cook, stirring frequently, for another 10 minutes. Reduce the heat to medium-low and continue to cook another 5 to 10 minutes, until the onions are deep golden brown. Stir in the thyme leaves and remove from the heat. Place in a bowl to cool. Store in an airtight container for up to 1 week in the fridge.

BACON JAM

PREP TIME: 15 minutes
COOK TIME: 20 minutes
CHILLING TIME: 1 hour
YIELD: Makes about 1½ cups (360 ml)

1½ pounds (680 g) sliced bacon, cut crosswise into 1-inch (2.5 cm) pieces
2 cups (300 g) finely chopped shallots
4 small cloves garlic, chopped
1 teaspoon single-origin chile powder
½ teaspoon mustard powder
½ cup (120 ml) bourbon
¼ cup (60 ml) maple syrup
⅓ cup (70 ml) sherry vinegar
⅓ cup (60 g) packed light brown sugar

Cook the bacon in a large skillet over medium-high heat until crispy. Reserving 1 tablespoon of fat in the pan, transfer the bacon to a plate. Depending on the size of your pan, you might have to do this in batches.

Add the shallots and garlic to the pan and cook, stirring, over medium heat for about 5 minutes, until translucent. Add the chile powder and mustard and cook, stirring, for 1 minute. Increase the heat to high and add the bourbon and maple syrup. Bring to a boil, scraping up the browned bits. Add the vinegar and brown sugar and return to a boil. Add the reserved bacon, reduce the heat to low, and simmer, stirring occasionally, for about 10 minutes, or until the liquid reduces to a thick glaze.

Transfer the mixture to a food processor and pulse until it has the consistency of a chunky jam. Cool completely and refrigerate in an airtight container for at least 1 hour. It will keep refrigerated for up to 4 weeks.

CHIPOTLE KETCHUP

PREP TIME: 10 minutes
COOK TIME: 1 hour
YIELD: Makes 2 cups (480 ml)

2 tablespoons olive oil
1 medium yellow onion, chopped
1 clove garlic, chopped
1 (28-ounce/794 g) can tomato puree
½ cup (100 g) packed light brown sugar
¼ cup (60 ml) apple cider vinegar
1 tablespoon tomato paste
1 teaspoon kosher salt
½ teaspoon mustard powder
½ teaspoon chipotle chile powder
2 teaspoons red pepper flakes
½ teaspoon cayenne pepper

Heat the oil in a medium saucepan over medium heat. Add the onion and cook for 5 to 8 minutes, until translucent. Stir in the garlic. Add the tomato puree, brown sugar, vinegar, tomato paste, salt, mustard, chipotle, red pepper flakes, and cayenne and stir to combine. Increase the heat to high and bring to a boil, then reduce the heat to low and simmer, stirring occasionally, for 45 to 60 minutes, until it is thick like ketchup. Using an immersion blender, food processor, or blender, puree the mixture until smooth.

Adjust the seasonings if needed and cool. Pour the ketchup into a container and seal. It can be refrigerated for up to 1 month.

PICO DE GALLO

PREP TIME: 10 minutes
YIELD: 2 cups (480 g)

1½ pounds (680 g) tomatoes cut into ¼- to ½-inch (6 to 12 mm) dice

½ large white onion, finely diced (about ¾ cup/95 g)

1 to 2 jalapeño chiles finely diced (seeds and membranes removed for a milder salsa)

½ cup (20 g) finely chopped fresh cilantro leaves

1 tablespoon fresh lime juice

Kosher salt

Place the tomatoes, onion, jalapeño, cilantro, and lime juice in a large bowl. Gently toss to combine. Taste and season with salt as needed. Add more jalapeño if you want a bit more zip.

GUACAMOLE

PREP TIME: 5 minutes
YIELD: 1½ cups (360 g)

4 Hass avocados, cut in half lengthwise and pitted

⅓ cup (40 g) finely chopped red onion

3 tablespoons chopped fresh chives

Juice of ½ lemon

Juice of ½ lime

2 teaspoons finely chopped jalapeño

Kosher salt and freshly cracked black pepper

Scoop the avocado flesh into a bowl. Add the onion, chives, lemon juice, lime juice, jalapeño, and salt and pepper to taste. Mash with a fork until half smooth and creamy. Taste and add more salt and pepper if desired.

TZATZIKI

PREP TIME: 10 minutes
YIELD: Serves 6 to 8

1½ cups (420 g) plain Greek yogurt

1 Persian cucumber, skin on, finely chopped (¾ to 1 cup/100 to 135 g)

Juice of 1 lemon, plus more if needed

3 cloves garlic, finely minced

2 tablespoons chopped fresh dill

Kosher salt and freshly cracked black pepper

Whisk together the yogurt, cucumber, lemon juice, garlic, and dill in a large bowl. Season with salt and pepper. Taste and adjust the salt, pepper, and/or lemon juice as needed. Serve immediately or store in an airtight container for up to 3 days.

SPICY MAYO

PREP TIME: 2 minutes
YIELD: ½ cup (120 ml)

½ cup (120 ml) mayonnaise

1 teaspoon sriracha

1 teaspoon minced garlic

1 teaspoon toasted sesame oil

1 teaspoon fresh lime juice

Salt and freshly ground black pepper

Whisk together the mayonnaise, sriracha, garlic, sesame oil, and lime juice in a small bowl and season with salt and pepper.

SPECIAL SAUCE

PREP TIME: 5 minutes
YIELD: Makes about ⅔ cup (170 ml)

½ cup (120 ml) mayonnaise
1 tablespoon sweet pickle relish
1 tablespoon ketchup
1 teaspoon Dijon mustard
1 clove garlic, grated on a Microplane
¼ teaspoon smoked paprika

¼ teaspoon onion powder
Pinch of red pepper flakes
Splash of Worcestershire sauce
Splash of hot sauce
Kosher salt and freshly ground black pepper, to taste

Whisk together all the ingredients in a small bowl. Taste and adjust as desired.

EXTRA-HERBY RANCH DRESSING

PREP TIME: 5 minutes
YIELD: Makes 1½ cups (360 ml)

½ cup (120 ml) mayonnaise
½ cup (120 ml) sour cream
½ cup (120 ml) buttermilk
1 teaspoon dried dill
1 teaspoon dried parsley
1 teaspoon dried chives

½ teaspoon garlic powder
¼ teaspoon onion powder
½ teaspoon kosher salt
½ teaspoon freshly cracked black pepper
Juice of 1 lemon

Whisk together the mayonnaise, sour cream, and buttermilk in a medium bowl until smooth. Add the dill, parsley, chives, garlic powder, onion powder, salt, and pepper and whisk until combined. Add the lemon juice and whisk again. Pour into a jar and chill in the refrigerator until ready to serve. It keeps refrigerated for up to 1 week.

MEAT RUB

PREP TIME: 5 minutes
YIELD: Makes 14 tablespoons

2 tablespoons freshly cracked black pepper
2 tablespoons ground white pepper
1 tablespoon cayenne pepper
1 tablespoon granulated onion
4 tablespoons granulated garlic
4 tablespoons kosher salt

EXTRA SPICES YOU CAN ADD:
1 tablespoon chipotle chile powder
1 tablespoon chile powder
1 tablespoon ground cumin
1 tablespoon smoked paprika
1 tablespoon dried oregano

Combine the spices in a small bowl and whisk together. Store in an airtight container for up to 3 months.

BBQ SAUCE VINAIGRETTE

PREP TIME: 5 minutes
YIELD: 1 cup (240 ml)

½ cup (120 ml) your favorite store-bought BBQ sauce
6 tablespoons apple cider vinegar
⅓ cup (70 ml) mild olive oil
2 teaspoons honey

1 small shallot, minced
1 clove garlic, minced
½ teaspoon hot sauce
Kosher salt and freshly ground black pepper

Combine the BBQ sauce, vinegar, oil, honey, shallot, garlic, and hot sauce in a medium bowl. Taste and season with salt and pepper as needed.

COMPOUND BUTTERS 101

PREP TIME: 10 minutes   **YIELD:** Makes about ¾ cup (180 g) each

To make each compound butter: Combine the butter with the remaining ingredients in a medium bowl. Stir to fully incorporate the ingredients. Keep it at room temperature if you plan to serve it the same day. Otherwise, transfer to a container and refrigerate for up to 5 days or freeze indefinitely.

CHIVE LEMON BUTTER

½ cup (115 g/1 stick) unsalted butter, at room temperature
¼ cup (12 g) chopped fresh chives
½ teaspoon kosher salt

½ teaspoon freshly ground black pepper
Zest of 1 lemon

SPICED MISO BUTTER

½ cup (115 g/1 stick) unsalted butter, at room temperature
2 tablespoons white miso

1 tablespoon sriracha
1½ teaspoons fresh lemon juice

BASIL CAPER BUTTER

½ cup (115 g/1 stick) unsalted butter, at room temperature
¼ cup (20 g) chopped fresh basil
½ teaspoon kosher salt

½ teaspoon freshly ground black pepper
1 tablespoon chopped capers

CHIPOTLE LIME BUTTER

½ cup (115 g/1 stick) unsalted butter, at room temperature
2 tablespoons chopped chipotle chiles in adobo

½ teaspoon kosher salt
Zest of 1 lime

AIOLI 101

PREP TIME: 10 minutes
YIELD: Makes about 1 cup (240 ml)

1 large egg
2 tablespoons fresh lemon juice
2 cloves garlic, chopped
½ teaspoon kosher salt
Pinch of freshly ground black pepper
½ cup (120 ml) avocado oil
½ cup (120 ml) canola oil

OPTIONAL ADD-INS:
Basil
Chives
Garlic

Combine the egg, lemon juice, garlic, salt, and pepper in a blender. Blend, starting on low speed to combine, then slowly increase the speed to high and blend for 30 seconds. Slowly add the oils in a thin stream through the hole in the lid until the aioli thickens. Stop the blender and scrape down the sides of the container. Blend for an additional 30 seconds, or until smooth and emulsified.

Place the aioli in a container, cover, and refrigerate for up to 1 week.

CREAMY KIMCHI POTATO SALAD

PREP TIME: 15 minutes
CHILLING TIME: 4 to 12 hours
COOK TIME: 15 minutes
YIELD: Serves 6

3 pounds (1.4 kg) baby new potatoes, halved or quartered
Kosher salt
1 cup (150 g) kimchi with its juices
¼ cup (60 ml) neutral oil, such as avocado or grapeseed
2 teaspoons toasted sesame oil
2 tablespoons rice vinegar
1 tablespoon honey
2 cloves garlic, crushed
½ teaspoon red pepper flakes

¾ cup (180 ml) mayonnaise
Freshly ground black pepper
8 slices bacon, cooked and crumbled
½ cup (75 g) kimchi, chopped (no extra juice)
1¼ cups (125 g) finely chopped celery
1 cup (135 g) frozen peas, thawed
8 green onions, thinly sliced (reserve some of the green tops for garnish)
2 teaspoons toasted sesame seeds

Place the potatoes in a large pot of salted water and bring to a boil. Cook for about 15 minutes, or until fork-tender. Drain, transfer to a large bowl, and let cool slightly, about 5 minutes.

Combine 1 cup (150 g) of the kimchi with juices, the oils, vinegar, honey, garlic, red pepper flakes, and mayonnaise in a blender and blend until smooth. Taste and season with salt and black pepper.

Pour the blended mixture over the cooked potatoes and add the bacon, ½ cup (75 g) chopped kimchi, the celery, peas, and most of the green onions. Stir to combine. Refrigerate for at least 4 hours or up to 12 hours. Serve garnished with green onion tops and sesame seeds.

MARINADES

LEMON HERB
PREP TIME: 10 minutes
YIELD: Makes about 1½ cups (360 ml)

Zest and juice of 2 large lemons
6 cloves garlic, finely chopped or grated
6 tablespoons olive oil
2 tablespoons finely chopped fresh oregano
2 tablespoons finely chopped fresh rosemary
2 tablespoons finely chopped fresh thyme
1 teaspoon red pepper flakes
Kosher salt and freshly ground black pepper

Combine all the ingredients in a high-powered blender and blend until smooth. Marinate chicken, steak, or pork for at least 1 hour and up to 12 hours. You don't want to marinate too long with a lemon marinade, as the acid from the citrus will eat away at the meat.

MOJO
PREP TIME: 10 minutes
YIELD: Makes about 1¼ cups (300 ml)

6 cloves garlic, peeled
1 medium shallot, roughly chopped
2 teaspoons kosher salt
Zest of 1 lime (about 2 teaspoons)
1½ teaspoons ground cumin
1 teaspoon dried oregano
½ teaspoon freshly ground black pepper
½ cup (120 ml) orange juice
⅓ cup (70 ml) fresh lime juice
⅓ cup (70 ml) olive oil

Combine all the marinade ingredients in a high-powered blender and blend until smooth. Marinate chicken, steak, or pork for at least 1 hour and up to 24 hours.

TERIYAKI-ISH MARINADE
PREP TIME: 10 minutes
YIELD: Makes about 1 cup (240 ml)

¼ cup (60 ml) olive oil
2 tablespoons light brown sugar
2 tablespoons apple cider vinegar
2 tablespoons soy sauce
2 tablespoons Worcestershire sauce
4 cloves garlic, finely diced
2 teaspoons chile powder
2 teaspoons ground cumin
2 teaspoons paprika
Kosher salt and freshly ground black pepper

In a high-powered blender, combine all the marinade ingredients and blend until smooth. Marinate chicken, steak, or pork for at least 1 hour and up to 24 hours.

Dinner party

WINE COUNTRY

We're weekending in wine country for this polished yet effortless take on grilling. As any good California girl knows, we're going to feature tons of fresh produce, plus decadent touches like grilled Brie and beef tenderloin drizzled with brown butter. Serve with your favorite wines and call it a free trip to Napa or Sonoma.

Grilled
BRIE AND GRAPES

PREP TIME: 20 minutes **MARINATING TIME:** 30 minutes **COOK TIME:** 8 minutes **YIELD:** Serves 4

Whisk together the vinegar, 3 tablespoons of the oil, the minced garlic, brown sugar, fennel seeds, and red pepper flakes in a large bowl. Season with salt and pepper, gently toss the grape clusters in the vinaigrette, and let sit for 30 minutes, tossing the grapes occasionally.

Preheat a gas or charcoal grill to medium-high heat (400°F to 450°F/205°C to 230°C) and lightly oil the grates.

Place the sliced baguette in a large bowl, drizzle with the remaining 2 tablespoons oil, and toss to coat. Season with salt and pepper.

Drizzle the cheese with oil and rub it around to coat. Remove the grapes and reserve the leftover vinaigrette.

Place the crostini, grapes, and cheese on the grill. Cook for 2 to 3 minutes, turning occasionally, until the crostini are toasty and charred. Remove from the grill to a platter and rub a clove of garlic on the toasted bread for extra flavor. Continue to cook the grapes for 3 to 5 minutes, until they are lightly charred. Remove grapes to the platter with the toasted bread. Continue to grill the cheese, turning as needed, until there are grill marks and the cheese is soft but not falling apart, 2 to 3 minutes per side. Add to the platter.

When ready to serve, drizzle the grapes and cheese with the reserved vinaigrette and serve with the crostini.

2 tablespoons red wine vinegar

5 tablespoons olive oil, plus more to oil the Brie

2 garlic cloves, 1 minced, 1 whole

1 tablespoon light brown sugar

1 teaspoon fennel seeds, crushed

Pinch of red pepper flakes

Kosher salt and freshly ground black pepper

2 to 3 clusters seedless red grapes

1 large baguette, sliced

1 (12- to 14-ounce/340 to 397 g) wheel Brie cheese

Brown Butter Grilled
BEEF TENDERLOIN

PREP TIME: 15 minutes   **COOK TIME:** 30 minutes   **YIELD:** Serves at least 8

---

1 teaspoon freshly ground black pepper

1 teaspoon garlic powder

1 teaspoon onion powder

1 teaspoon dried oregano

1 teaspoon dried basil

1 teaspoon dried thyme

1 teaspoon paprika

1 teaspoon red pepper flakes

1 teaspoon sugar

1 teaspoon fennel seeds, crushed

2 teaspoons sea salt

1 (2-pound/910 g) whole beef tenderloin

2 tablespoons olive oil

1 cup (230 g/2 sticks) unsalted butter, cut into pieces

2 tablespoons minced shallots

¼ cup (about 30 g) finely chopped fresh herbs, such as parsley, thyme, rosemary, and oregano

2 tablespoons capers, drained and rinsed

Combine the black pepper, garlic powder, onion powder, oregano, basil, thyme, paprika, red pepper flakes, sugar, fennel seeds, and salt in a small bowl and mix well.

Put the tenderloin on a plate or platter, pat it dry with paper towels, and rub the spice blend all over the beef, including the ends. Let sit at room temperature for 30 minutes.

Preheat a gas or charcoal grill to 500°F (260°C). Have a pair of tongs, a meat thermometer, a platter, and a piece of aluminum foil at the ready, close to your grill.

Right before cooking, rub the tenderloin with the oil. Place the tenderloin on the grill. Close the lid and cook undisturbed for 5 minutes. Turn the tenderloin over and cook with the lid down for an additional 5 minutes. Roll the tenderloin to one of the smaller sides (left or right sides) and cook for 3 minutes with the lid up. Cook the final smaller side in the same manner for 3 minutes. Transfer the tenderloin to the platter and insert the meat thermometer into the center of the meat. If the thermometer reads 110°F (40°C), the tenderloin is cooked perfectly, medium-rare. If it's not there yet, or you prefer a more well-done tenderloin, place it back onto the grill and retest it every minute until desired doneness is achieved.

Remove the tenderloin from the grill, cover it loosely with foil, and let it rest for 10 to 15 minutes.

Meanwhile, heat a medium skillet over medium heat. Add the butter and let it melt, then add the shallots and herbs and cook for 5 minutes. Add the capers and cook for 2 to 3 minutes, until the butter is lightly browned.

Slice the tenderloin into slices ½ inch (1.25 cm) thick and serve with the browned butter sauce.

Grilled ASPARAGUS

with Shaved Parmesan and Crumbled Grilled Prosciutto

PREP TIME: 5 minutes   **COOK TIME:** 10 minutes   **YIELD:** Serves 4

Preheat a gas or charcoal grill to medium-high heat (400°F to 450°F/205°C to 230°C) and lightly oil the grates.

Toss the asparagus with the oil, salt, and pepper to taste in a large bowl until evenly coated.

Place the asparagus onto the grill and cook for 8 to 10 minutes, flipping once halfway through, until the spears are tender yet still crisp.

While the asparagus is cooking, add the prosciutto to the grill and cook for 1 to 2 minutes per side, until lightly crisped. Remove the crisped prosciutto to a paper towel–lined plate and allow to cool, then crumble.

When the asparagus is done, remove from the grill and transfer to a serving platter. Sprinkle with the crumbled prosciutto and the cheese and serve.

1 pound (455 g) asparagus, trimmed

2 tablespoons olive oil

¼ teaspoon kosher salt

Freshly ground black pepper

2 ounces (57 g) prosciutto, thinly sliced

¼ cup (25 g) shaved Parmesan cheese

FARRO
and Summer
TOMATO SALAD

PREP TIME: 20 minutes   **COOK TIME:** 30 minutes   **YIELD:** Serves 4

---

1 cup (190 g) farro

3 cups (710 ml) water

1 tablespoon kosher salt

⅓ cup (70 ml) olive oil

3 tablespoons red wine vinegar

1 teaspoon Dijon mustard

1 large shallot, minced

1 clove garlic, minced

1 cup (100 g) cherry tomatoes,
    halved

2 heirloom tomatoes, cut into wedges

2 tablespoons chopped fresh
    oregano

2 tablespoons chopped fresh basil

2 tablespoons chopped fresh parsley

6 ounces (170 g) feta cheese,
    broken into large chunks

Kosher salt and freshly ground
    black pepper

Combine the farro, water, and salt in a medium saucepan and bring to a boil over medium-high heat. Reduce the heat to low, cover, and simmer for 30 minutes, or until the farro is tender. Drain well, then transfer to a large bowl to cool.

Meanwhile, whisk together the oil, vinegar, mustard, shallot, and garlic in a small bowl.

Add the tomatoes, oregano, basil, parsley, cheese, and vinaigrette to the farro. Season with salt and pepper. Serve immediately, or cover and refrigerate until ready to serve.

Buttermilk SHERBET

with Strawberries and Figs

PREP TIME: 20 minutes **COOK TIME:** 5 minutes **CHURNING TIME:** Manufacturer's recommendation
FREEZING TIME: 6 hours **MACERATING TIME:** 30 minutes **YIELD:** Serves 4 to 6

TO MAKE THE SHERBET: First make a simple syrup by combining the sugar and water in a small saucepan. Bring to a boil over medium-high heat, then lower the heat and simmer 2 to 3 minutes to dissolve the sugar. Remove from the heat and cool to room temperature.

Whisk together the buttermilk, simple syrup, lemon juice, vanilla bean paste, and kosher salt in a medium bowl. Place the mixture in the refrigerator to chill completely.

Pour the sherbet base into an ice cream maker and churn following the manufacturer's instructions. Pop in the freezer and freeze until firm, at least 6 hours.

TO MACERATE THE STRAWBERRIES AND FRESH FIGS: While the sherbet is firming up, whisk together the sugar, vinegar, orange zest, and sea salt in a medium bowl. Add the strawberries and figs and give it a stir. Let the mixture sit, stirring occasionally, for at least 30 minutes or up to 6 hours to allow the flavors to meld.

Scoop the sherbet into bowls and serve with the macerated strawberries and figs and crumbled shortbread.

FOR THE SHERBET:
¾ cup (150 g) granulated sugar
¾ cup (180 ml) water
3 cups (720 ml) low-fat buttermilk
Juice of 1 lemon
1½ teaspoons vanilla bean paste
Pinch of kosher salt

FOR THE MACERATED STRAWBERRIES AND FRESH FIGS:
3 tablespoons granulated sugar
1 teaspoon balsamic vinegar
1 teaspoon grated orange zest
Pinch of sea salt
1 pint (357 g) fresh strawberries, hulled and quartered
4 fresh figs, stems trimmed, quartered

Crushed shortbread cookies, for serving

ACKNOWLEDGMENTS

MY WGC FAMILY: It's safe to say that if it weren't for you, I wouldn't get to have the most fun of my life coming up with all these new recipes to share. It's truly a gift getting to do that, so thank you from the bottom of my heart for trusting me, believing in me, and showing up for me. Here's to many more tasty meals together!

MATT: Your talent knows no bounds. These memories are forever. Love you always. I'm so glad I adopted myself into your family all those years ago. You'll never be rid of me.

ADAM: Adam! Thank you for your ingenious ideas, making it all look so damn beautiful, and for not only coming along for the ride but also keeping all the wheels on the bus. You complete me. I can't wait to open up a bakery together and live our best lives off the grid one day!

AMY: You literally make my dreams come true because you take all my crazy ideas and turn them into gorgeously styled reality. Thank you for being there with me every day.

HOLLY: Our captain and leader. Thank you for advocating for me every step of the way, but most of all, thanks for making sure these books get out into the world as beautifully as they do.

JANIS: Once again you've made sure that I've made it out the other side in one piece. Part of what makes this process so rewarding is knowing that I have the support I need, and you give me that invaluable peace of mind.

RACHEL: I don't know how you do it, but your ability to climb inside my mind and perfectly capture my voice is truly unmatched. A million thank-yous for helping me say everything that I want to say and for making sure I sound semi-intelligent along the way!

SOPHIE: You're a legend! Thank you for everything you did on the front end of this book and the shoot weeks! Plus, I am blown away by your ability to crush a photo shoot and then go home to entertain your friends. You're basically a superhero, and I'd like some of that energy!!

DIANA, WADE, AND ELLE: Once again, thank you for the good vibes and good times. You help me forget that this is actually work! I love being in the studio with our whole crew.

BRITTNEY: You are the hair and makeup gift that keeps on giving. Thank you for helping me feel even more like myself—just a touch better.

ZACK: You've been such a big part of my life that having an entire chapter in one of my books only feels right. Thank you for all the guidance, support, and hangovers.

LILY AND ALEX: Working with the two of you has been an absolute dream. Having both of you in my corner is everything I could have hoped for and more; I can't wait to see what we continue to accomplish together. I'm obsessed with our little powerhouse trio!

And a huge shout-out to all of my favorite brands that I continuously reach for and that keep me feeling inspired in the kitchen. Tillamook, thank you for making the most incredible cheese and ice cream known to man, for only using the best ingredients, and for doing meltable cheese so, so right. Maldon, thank you for being the best in the flavor and texture game. I'd say it's alarming how much of your flaky salt I go through, but it really is the perfect amount. Stella Artois, thank you for keeping my fridge stocked and any hour happy hour. It's been a dream come true to work with you—cheers to us! And to the Hollywood Farmers' Market and all the vendors, I can't share enough of my gratitude for supplying me with the most gorgeous produce week after week. We love you forever and ever.

TO MY FRIENDS BOTH NEAR AND FAR:
One of the biggest challenges to sharing new and exciting recipes is inspiration. But when I think about all the delicious meals I want to treat you to, I'm never short on inspiration. Thank you for filling my table and my life with your joy, love, and appetite. And for always answering my phone calls and FaceTimes. I know my obsessive calling can be overwhelming to some of you, so thank you for letting me be me.

MOM, DAD, AND ANYA: With each incredible accomplishment in my life—and a fifth cookbook is most certainly among the tippy top of them—I can't help but credit all of you. You have given me the strength and unwavering sense of self that allows me to chase my dreams. I can reach higher because you're there to lift me up. I love you so much.

THOMAS: If you'd asked me five years ago whether we'd ever make it here AND be working together as partners AND have a toddler AND still want to spend time together . . . I'd plead the fifth. But here we are! You are the M&M's to my cookies and the cheese to my nachos. It just wouldn't be as good without you. I love you forever!

POPPY: What can I say? You turned my world upside down, and it's never looked better. You're the best kitchen sidekick and fiercest food critic I've ever had (I live for those five-star ratings from you!), and you inspire me to keep growing and challenging myself because I know you're there watching me and cheering me on every step of the way. Love you the most most!

INDEX

Editor: Holly Dolce
Designer: Claudia Wu
Design Manager: Danielle Youngsmith
Managing Editor: Annalea Manalili
Production Managers: Kathleen Gaffney and Denise LaCongo

Library of Congress Control Number: 2023946472

ISBN: 978-1-4197-7182-8
eISBN: 979-8-88707-208-1

Printed and bound in China
10 9 8 7 6 5 4 3 2 1

Abrams books are available at special discounts when purchased in quantity
for premiums and promotions as well as fundraising or educational use.
Special editions can also be created to specification. For details, contact
specialsales@abramsbooks.com or the address below.

Abrams® is a registered trademark of Harry N. Abrams, Inc.

ABRAMS The Art of Books
195 Broadway, New York, NY 10007
abramsbooks.com